ISLE OF MAN AT WAR 1939–45

ISLE OF MAN AT WAR 1939–45

Matthew Richardson

Pen & Sword
MILITARY

First published in Great Britain in 2018 by
PEN & SWORD MILITARY
An imprint of
Pen & Sword Books Ltd
Yorkshire – Philadelphia

Copyright © Matthew Richardson, 2018

ISBN 978 1 52672 073 3

Printed and bound in England by CPI Group (UK) Ltd, Croydon, CR0 4YY

Pen & Sword Books Limited incorporates the imprints of Atlas, Archaeology, Aviation, Discovery, Family History, Fiction, History, Maritime, Military, Military Classics, Politics, Select, Transport, True Crime, Air World, Frontline Publishing, Leo Cooper, Remember When, Seaforth Publishing, The Praetorian Press, Wharncliffe Local History, Wharncliffe Transport, Wharncliffe True Crime and White Owl.

For a complete list of Pen & Sword titles please contact

PEN & SWORD BOOKS LIMITED
47 Church Street, Barnsley, South Yorkshire, S70 2AS, England
E-mail: enquiries@pen-and-sword.co.uk
Website: www.pen-and-sword.co.uk

Or
PEN AND SWORD BOOKS
1950 Lawrence Rd, Havertown, PA 19083, USA
E-mail: Uspen-and-sword@casematepublishers.com
Website: www.penandswordbooks.com

CONTENTS

Acknowledgements

There are many people for whose help with the preparation of this book I remain deeply indebted. In particular I must thank those who lived through the Second World War and who helped me directly with my research. Bob Quayle provided me with vivid insights into his experiences in the army and afterwards. Gordon Cowley was equally helpful regarding his experiences in the Royal Marines. Frank Cowin and Terry Cringle assisted me with aspects relating to the home front. Hector Duff gave me access to his marvellous collection of personal photographs and allowed me to transcribe his memories of active service. It is a point that I have made before in other books which I have written, but it bears repetition: I remain deeply aware of the debt that my generation owes to theirs.

I must also thank those who provided family papers or photographs and who allowed me to use material relating to their forebears, in no particular order: John Hall, Alistair Ramsay, Sarah Clucas, Dawn Beck, Junemary Moyle, Bernard Scarffe, John Caley, Lynda Cannell, the Quirk family, the staff of Kirk Michael Fire Station, Cathy Clucas, and of course Jack and Helen Cain who allowed me to use material relating to Helen's father Dusty Miller.

Likewise Barry Bridson, who has helped me in my work for many years, deserves special mention. Perhaps unusually for a collector of militaria, he is acutely aware of the historical significance of this material for the Isle of Man. My perennial friend Andy Wint also deserves credit for his help. Stephen Fogden assisted me with research and photographs, as did Ivor Ramsden of the Manx Aviation and Preservation Society (MAPS). Dr Sue Nicol assisted me with research on Norwegians on the Isle of Man, and colleagues Alan Franklin and Yvonne Cresswell provided advice on internment aspects.

Matthew Richardson
Douglas
Isle of Man, 2017

Introduction

The book you are about to read is one that I had wanted to write for a number of years but which, if I am completely honest, I had balked at tackling. The subject seemed so enormous that I felt it would be almost impossible to do justice to it. It was only when an opportunity arose through Pen & Sword Books that finally I decided that it was time to act and put those doubts to one side. Accordingly I would like to thank Roni Wilkinson, design manager at Pen & Sword, for his ongoing faith in my abilities and for presenting me with this challenge.

During the many years that I have lived on the Isle of Man I have met numbers of people who served here during the war, or who were born on the island and lived through the 1939–45 period. Each has offered me a slightly different facet of the story, so that over the course of time I was able mentally to put together an image of what was happening to the island and its people during those momentous years. Some of those people are mentioned in the acknowledgements section of the book but many more are not; this is because these were in many cases only fleeting acquaintances or chance encounters, but they all added a vital element.

Indeed, all helped with the process of forming the outline of the book in my mind. Many of those facets will be described as the story unfolds, from the Steam Packet crews at Dunkirk to the Manx Regiment going off to war in North Africa, the farmer toiling under wartime regulations, the interned German, and the airman (or woman) stationed at one of the island's airfields. It is also important to remember that so much of what took place here was highly secret so that details of it have only emerged in recent decades, but it is fair to say that the Isle of Man bristled with weaponry during those six years. The best term I heard anyone who was here use to describe it was that 'the Island was an armed camp.' So much of this activity was directed towards training and preparing people for confrontation with the enemy, or was vital 'behind-the-scenes' work which nevertheless contributed to victory.

Wherever possible I have tried to allow the people who were there at the time to tell this story in their own words, and have acted merely as the facilitator enabling them to do this. I hope that I have gone some way in this book towards conveying that sense of bustle and activity which characterizes the war years on the Isle of Man.

CHAPTER ONE

1939: Who Will Win?

While the outbreak of war in 1914 had taken many people by surprise, there was almost a sense of inevitability about the conflict that broke out twenty-five years later. The warning signs had been apparent to anyone who cared to look, and certainly from the time of the Munich Crisis Hitler's ambition and lust for expansion were obvious. Early in 1939 the Lieutenant Governor Lord Granville had issued a booklet asking the people of the Isle of Man to register for voluntary service in whatever capacity they could. In addition to the Territorial Army, volunteers were needed for the Loyal Manx Association (which supported the police as special constables), and Auxiliary Fire Service, as well as assisting at Noble's hospital or on the land to increase agricultural output. However, it was perceived to the dismay of many that the outlook of Tynwald was still one of 'it won't happen here.'

In June of that year, the shape of things to come was made glaringly apparent to the people of the island during the famous TT motorcycle races. It was without doubt the most politicized meeting ever to have taken place in the history of the event, and the swastika flying among the other national flags above the

> **15 MINUTES ONLY**
>
> separates Manxland from England by air—and in England they are preparing for the safety of the public from air attacks.
>
> The Manx Government are doing nothing whatever for your safety.
>
> Ask your Member of the Keys about it.

In the early part of 1939 there was growing concern that the Isle of Man was ill-prepared for war. This editorial comment is from the Isle of Man Times *of 4 February that year.*

grandstand was an ominous portent. The Germans had fielded a national team that year, with the express intention of securing a propaganda victory for Hitler and the Nazis. Such was the media profile of the TT at this time that it would rank alongside the 1936 Berlin Olympics and the world heavyweight boxing title in terms of sporting coups achieved by Germany in these years. German army dispatch rider Georg Meier stormed to victory aboard a supercharged BMW in the Senior race, a task made all the easier because British rivals Norton were by now so heavily engaged in war work that they did not field a team and handed their machines to privateers. As a reward, Meier was promoted by Hitler to the rank of lieutenant. Earlier in the week, the Italian team of Benelli had taken victory in the Lightweight race, and the news was cabled

Cartoonist Dusty Miller captures the mood of the 1939 TT as a three-cornered fight, with Adolf Hitler and Mussolini competing against John Bull. The title was 'Who Will Win?'. (Courtesy of Helen and Jack Cain)

directly to Mussolini in Rome. Only in the Junior race was British pride maintained, with a win by British firm Velocette (albeit with an Irishman, Stanley Woods, in the saddle).

On 24 August 1939 the island's only Territorial Army formation, the 15th (Isle of Man) Light Anti-Aircraft Regiment Royal Artillery, was mobilized for permanent service, a clear sign of the worsening political situation. The unit had been in existence for just over a year, since the expansion of the Territorial Army by the Westminster government in 1938, and though the response of young Manxmen had been heartening with three batteries recruited remarkably quickly, at the time of mobilization its new drill hall at Tromode was not even finished. A parallel development, the construction of a new airfield at Jurby as part of the RAF expansion scheme,

Irish TT rider Stanley Woods. He scored the only British win at the 1939 TT races, riding a Velocette. The Senior trophy was won by BMW, while the Lightweight was taken back to Italy by Benelli. (Author's collection)

was nearer completion. Thousands of tons of spoil from the Laxey mines deads had been transported in a fleet of lorries in order to level the site, and to provide hardcore for the runways. RAF Jurby would be open within a matter of weeks.

After years of simmering tension, the German invasion of Poland on 1 September was to be the final straw, and when the Führer refused to accede to the Anglo-French ultimatum and withdraw his troops, on 3 September Great Britain found herself once again at war. The first casualty on the Isle of Man was that September's Manx Grand Prix meeting, which was immediately cancelled, with the Manx Motor Cycle Club suffering a heavy

WHERE THE 'ELL ARE WE ?

Oh lor luv a duck! Hi! Come 'ere, Bill, an' see
This 'ere book wot the Gover'ment's sent.
It says "We'll be eager to share in defence!"
Lumme! Eager!—and who'll pay me rent?

The last time I went, I was eager enough,
An' I joined up all swellin' with pride—
'Till I found that we lads were out fightin' like 'ell
To defend profiteers' dirty 'ide.

An' wot of the wife, an' the kids? Listen, Bill,
They were told to "buzz off to the shore,"
While some damned 'ole stale records wot nobody wants
Could 'ave cellars and shelters galore!

Then there's that Committee wot sat months ago—
Are they sleepin' an' snorin' there still?
No shelters! No gas masks! My God!—an' I would
Put 'em all "on the square" with Ol' Bill!

We're right "in the cart," in a 'ell of a mess,
While a lawyer chap loses 'is jaw
An' he bleats like a Prophet Elijah, to-day,
"That he doesn't think there'll be no war."

No gas masks—no shelters—they're not needed 'ere?
Cripes! I'm bustin' me buttons with smiles!
Then wot do they mean when they're askin' for men
For "to share in defence of these Isles"?
                                              M.

Another Dusty cartoon shows two ex-servicemen discussing the approaching conflict.

financial loss as a result. The same month and also as a consequence of the outbreak of war the island's first civil aerodrome, Hall Caine airfield near Ramsey, was closed (though it was shortly to be taken over as a satellite airfield for RAF Jurby). It was then used as a Relief Landing Ground, and to support air-to-air gunnery target towing operations. The target towing aircraft would overfly Hall Caine at 2,000ft, heading out to the ranges over Ramsey Bay. After the trainee air gunners had done their best, the target towing aircraft (usually a Fairey Battle, Hawker Henley or Westland Wallace) would fly back to Hall Caine and drop the drogue over the airfield. A control officer was deployed from Jurby to oversee operations and report the 'scores' back by telephone. Later, with the opening of RAF Andreas in 1941, Hall Caine would cease to be used as a Relief Landing Ground, but it would continue to support the target towing operations for a while. Later still, after the RAF vacated the airfield, it would be obstructed to prevent possible use by enemy aircraft.

As in the previous conflict, on the outbreak of war the Royal Navy requisitioned some of the Isle of Man Steam Packet fleet, notably the *King Orry* which as in the First World War became

Members of the 15th Light Anti-Aircraft Regiment (Manx Regiment) parade past the Lieutenant Governor Lord Granville around the time of the regiment's mobilization. (Courtesy of the Manx Aviation Preservation Society/Manx Regiment Museum)

HMS *King Orry*. Most of her crew were replaced by Royal Navy personnel, with the exception of her engineering staff who were retained because of their familiarity with the ship's engines. Only the *Rushen Castle* and *Peveril* continued to provide a regular link with the UK, as most of the other ships were chartered by the Admiralty. Retaining their Manx crews, they were kept busy as troopships, ferrying the soldiers of the British Expeditionary Force (BEF) to France under its commander Field Marshal Lord Gort VC.

For those who were old enough to remember, it was all vividly redolent of the previous conflict with Germany twenty-five years earlier. Under the headline 'My Boy is Off to France', one newspaper carried an account by a proud but worried Douglas father of his son's departure for the front in October:

> I gripped his hand...
> 'Goodbye my boy, and good luck!'
> 'Goodbye dad,' he answered...
> 'Goodbye mum.'
> And then a bit shyly – 'Give me a kiss. I know I'm a man now, but I feel somehow I'd like a kiss from you. It's only been a short leave home, but now I'm off – don't know where exactly, but most likely the front line, as I'm in the infantry...

A final handshake...

> 'Goodbye son, I know you'll have courage to carry out your duty.'
>
> The door closed, and he was gone.
>
> I, who am left, will be with him in thought, and will follow him in imagination.[1]

Conscription arrived on the island in the same month, and men of suitable age were required to register for service in the armed forces at Ramsey, Peel, Castletown and Douglas. Compulsory military service had been introduced in the United Kingdom as early as May 1939, but an attempt by the lieutenant governor to push legislation extending it to the Isle of Man through the House of Keys shortly afterwards had failed. Many MHKs had objected to the lack of consultation, with the Manx Labour Party particularly opposed. However, in October 1939 a motion to adopt compulsory military service along United Kingdom lines was passed, with several Labour members now speaking in support. The Manx legislation adopted the same system of reserved occupations and exemptions as the UK, the principle being that every male of military age had to register, and the local tribunal would then decide if they would best serve the war effort by remaining in their own job or joining the armed forces. An attempted anti-conscription rally in Peel in November met with little sympathy from the local population, but a similar meeting in Colby attracted around 100 people. After they were blocked from using the Level Hall over fears that the meeting contravened the Defence of the Realm Act, it went ahead outside. The speakers, a mixture of Manx Labour Party members and conscientious objectors, were all at pains to stress that they did not object to conscription as such, but rather the 'undemocratic' way in which it had been introduced to the Isle of Man. More concerning for the authorities was the fact that when the first Manx cohort to be called up was medically examined, it was found that 70 per cent were classified as Grade 1, whereas the equivalent in England was 80 per cent; a worrying indictment of Manx public health.

With the coming of autumn, blackout restrictions began to make themselves felt, sometimes with humorous consequences: vehicles travelling at night had to have masks fitted to their headlights, and this coupled with the fact that all road signs had been removed in order to delay an invading enemy, led to many confusing incidents. On one occasion a driver from Ramsey who thought he was heading south towards Castletown found himself at the Point of Ayre.

As Christmas approached, there was a feeling of pride among many that a fund had already been established through which to send a present to every Manx serviceman who was away from home at that time. Overall, however, there was a sense of uncertainty as to how the war would affect the island. The insular government was in receipt of income tax revenues from the previous year, but no one could be certain what incomes would be like in the year to come. Individuals also were apprehensive about the way in which new wartime regulations and restrictions would affect themselves and their businesses. Perhaps the biggest development politically was the establishment of Tynwald's War Committee, as a reflection of the Cabinet style of government in Westminster. However, the fact that it was centred around the lieutenant governor was testament to the authority that the post still carried in the Isle of Man at the time.

THE DEEMSTER COWLEY (Chairman).
Left to right—J. R. CORRIN, m.l.c.; A. E. KITTO, m.h.k.; D. J. TEARE, m.h.k.; R. G. JOHNSON (Secretary); A. J TEARE, m.h.k.; W. C. CRAINE, m.h.k.; S. NORRIS, m.h.k.

The War Committee of Tynwald. The establishment of the committee laid the foundations for the ministerial form of government that would emerge on the Isle of Man in the post-war years.

CHAPTER TWO

1940: A Great Armed Camp

The year 1940 is widely regarded as one of the darkest hours in British history. Following the collapse of France, for the first time since the Norman Conquest (or perhaps the Spanish Armada) the country had been in serious danger of invasion. Yet amid the darkness there was a glimmer of light – the 'miracle of Dunkirk' – which saved the BEF and kept Britain in the war. The Isle of Man played more than a fair part in this great undertaking; at the same time providing accommodation for the many thousands of enemy aliens who were to be arrested as potential threats to national security. In addition, the island would send reinforcements and recruits for the army and act as a training ground for thousands of others.

The year began quietly enough though. This was the era of the 'Phoney War', when on the ground there was no actual fighting as each side eyed the other warily. For people on the Isle of Man, their immediate concern was closer to home. With the harsh experience of the First World War still fresh in the minds of many, particular importance was attached to finding substitute industries which could potentially replace the expected shortfall in income from tourism. An early but short-lived wartime Manx industry was net-making. Upon the outbreak of war the Ministry of Supply had announced the urgent need for camouflage nets to obscure military hardware from the air. It believed that coastal regions might be best placed to respond to this through their already established industries producing fishing nets. In February 1940, Dowty's of Castle Hill in Douglas secured a contract to produce 6,500 nets and subcontracted the work to other parts of the island. Of particular note was the net-making factory that sprang up in Port St Mary, using mainly female labour, in order to supply Dowty's. This was considered important because in the previous war, working-class women had suffered the worst hardship following the collapse of the tourist industry. Other similar initiatives involved the setting-up of a cottage industry in the south of the island producing crocheted gloves, which had once been supplied from Czechoslovakia. In the event, however, net-making lasted less than a year and did not prove to be the panacea that many had hoped it would.

As far as the British army was concerned, camouflage nets were not the only item in short supply. A lack of weapons affected many of the recently-raised Territorial formations. In France,

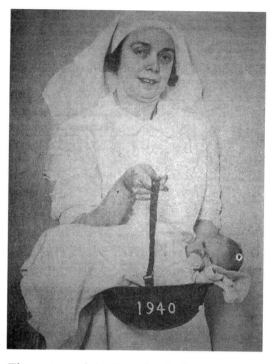

The matron of the Jane Crookall Maternity Home in Douglas with the first war baby of 1940.

however, the problem faced by the BEF was not simply dearth of hardware or equipment, though future Field Marshal Bernard Montgomery later said that it was in no fit state to undertake a realistic exercise, let alone fight a major European war. The deeper malaise was that the British had gone to France in 1939 prepared to fight the war that had ended in 1918. They immediately began digging trenches, in some cases on the same positions they had occupied when the last conflict ended. Although the British had pioneered tank tactics in the First World War, in the interwar years any official interest in armoured warfare had withered to almost nothing. By contrast, the Germans in the 1930s had devoured every British pamphlet or doctrine on tank warfare that they could find. Two men in particular, Generals Heinz Guderian and Erwin Rommel, would become supreme experts in combining air power

Dutch soldiers recover the wreckage of the Hurricane in which Pilot Officer George Slee of Santon was shot down in May 1940. Serving with 17 Squadron RAF, he was involved in a dogfight over the coast of Holland. (Courtesy of H.J. Nootenboom)

and armour, and the British would pay a heavy price for their neglect.

On 10 May 1940, the 'Phoney War' came to an end. German tanks and infantry rolled into the Low Countries. The French were determined that as far as possible this war would be fought on the soil of Belgium rather than France, and so they and the British left their carefully-prepared positions constructed over the winter and sallied forth to meet the threat, except that it was a ruse. The real German thrust came further south through the Ardennes: densely-wooded country that the French believed to be unsuited to armour. The French army, low in morale and riven with defeatism, collapsed. The BEF, trapped by the German pincer, together with some French units began to retreat towards Dunkirk. On 26 May a decision was taken by the British War Cabinet that the situation was critical and the BEF must be evacuated. The French high command was still proposing offensives using formations that had either been destroyed already or whose morale had evaporated, but saving what remained of Britain's army now became Gort's priority. Admiral Bertram Ramsay was given the task of planning the withdrawal, which became known as Operation DYNAMO.

Ramsay's main problem, however, was that Dunkirk, formerly France's third port and possessed of no fewer than seven dock basins, had been subjected to relentless German bombing since 18 May. The town was now a shambles. The oil refinery that stood at the entrance to the main harbour was blazing fiercely, providing a beacon for friend and foe alike. The bulk of Ramsay's evacuation was initially planned to take place from the beaches outside the town, which could only be approached by shallow-draught vessels. To facilitate this, trucks were driven out to sea as far as possible and the roofs planked over by the Royal Engineers to create makeshift jetties. However, it was soon realized that the East Mole (or breakwater) of Dunkirk harbour could be used as an emergency landing-stage. It was not intended for mooring and getting alongside the Mole was not easy, but the advantage it offered was that large-draught vessels could come alongside it and they could carry thousands rather than hundreds of troops.

Lance Corporal Beaumont, a son-in-law of Mrs J. Cowell of Windsor Café, Port Erin, had joined the army in January 1940. He was drafted to France a fortnight later and moved to Belgium when the enemy invasion of that country took place. With little of the necessary equipment but fighting with unfaltering resolution, his detachment endured the perils of withdrawal to the sand dunes at Bray (8 miles from Dunkirk) and eventually reached the town itself. Subjected to terrible gunfire and bombing attacks from land and air, they assisted in carrying the wounded into the town. The Mole was incessantly bombed and smashed in places, but was hurriedly repaired so as to enable the transfer of the dying and wounded to hospital ships and other vessels en route from England, a task that was accomplished mainly at night. The human cost of the war was apparent to Beaumont, who stated in a letter home that 'The real heroes of Dunkirk are the men who have laid down their lives in this terrible holocaust and devastation in the interests of liberty, justice and truth.'[1]

As the evacuation continued, Admiral Ramsay requisitioned as much civilian shipping as he could, and a number of Isle of Man Steam Packet Company ships that had been used by the

Royal Navy to transport troops to France were now chartered to bring them home. They were not commandeered but were hired, along with whatever crews they had on board at the time. This is an important detail, in the light of later events. However, two other ships had already been taken directly into the Royal Navy. HMS *King Orry* had been acting as an armed boarding vessel in the Channel, searching ships for contraband intended for Germany, and HMS *Mona's Isle* had performed a similar role. Numbers of Manx crewmen remained aboard these ships, but did so as naval reservists rather than civilians.

The first Manx ship into Dunkirk at the beginning of the evacuation was HMS *Mona's Isle*. Her crew at this time was probably half-and-half Manx naval reservists who had been part of her crew before the war and regular Royal Navy sailors. One of the latter group, Sub Lieutenant Denys Thorp, has left us a remarkable account of that first trip into the inferno. Thorp was

SS Mona's Isle, *seen prior to the war. As HMS* Mona's Isle *she was badly damaged by air attack while leaving Dunkirk in May 1940. (Author's collection)*

an RNVR officer and had joined HMS *Mona's Isle* in September 1939. He wrote later of the ship's arrival in the early hours of the morning:

> The scene in the port was depressing in the extreme, partly owing to the artificial darkness due to the smoke. There was a good deal of bomb damage and debris and the only signs of activity were a number of French labourers picking over the debris to see what they could find. Astern of us was a British destroyer looking very dirty and battle-stained. At about 0530 the troops began to arrive and we were told to take as many as we could and take them back to Dover when the ship was full. When they did arrive there seemed to be an endless stream, no wounded but they were dog tired and dirty and looked as though they had been through many ordeals. There were many from many different units, officers and men separated. They came on board in an orderly stream and distributed themselves about the ship. I remember being approached by one young officer who told me that the general would be arriving shortly and would like a bath. I had to break it to him that we had no bath on board. However, when he did appear I found a berth for him in the chart room and felt very sorry for him as he was obviously suffering from great strain.[2]

He continued with a description of an air attack on the *Mona's Isle* during her return passage:

> Our anti-aircraft armament consisted of one 12-pounder aft and a pair of Lewis guns on each wing of the bridge. I was near the port Lewis gun when the aircraft were identified as enemy and opened fire on them as they peeled off. This was not however effective. Most of the attacking runs were made from the starboard quarter and our view was thus obscured. The Lewis-gunner had by this time taken over and I was acting as loader. The next thing that happened was a violent explosive crack in our immediate vicinity and I found myself lying on the deck together with the Lewis-gunner. He said 'Are you all right, sir?' and I said 'Yes, are you?' and he said he thought he was. So I said well, we had better get on with it, so we continued firing

at what targets presented themselves. It was apparent that a cannon shell had passed between us and hit a stanchion a couple of feet behind us. The aircraft circled round until their ammunition was exhausted and then flew off towards the coast. To say I was glad to see the last of them is an understatement. Everyone was suffering from shock in a greater or less degree but nobody on the bridge was injured except the quartermaster who pulled a piece of wood from the back of his head and carried on with the job. The 1st Lieutenant and I left the bridge to survey the damage in order to report to the Captain the situation. When I went down I was appalled by the scene and the condition of the ship. With so many men on board, perhaps half of them on the upper and shelter decks, it is not surprising that there were so many casualties. It was estimated that there were about thirty killed outright and sixty more or less seriously injured. Of the ship's company one officer was wounded by shell fragments in the leg, and one rating was killed while standing outside the chart room door. If he had lain down, his life would have been saved.

Four or five ratings were wounded. Petty Officer Pope RNR, though badly wounded in the wrist, closed some ready-use lockers in the 12-pounder enclosure after the 12-pounder crew was knocked out, in the face of heavy machine-gun and cannon fire and afterwards received the DSC. The plight of the wounded soldiers was more tragic as after what they had endured in France, they came aboard this ship thankful to be in the Navy's care and bound for home, with the feeling that their troubles were for the moment at an end. I was very upset by this aspect at the time and it took me a long time to forget that no doctor was carried and no sick bay attendant, but their mates came to their help and did what they could for them. The ship was in a sorry state and when the damage was assessed the situation did not look too bright. It was found that the tele-motor pipes were severed and the ship could not be steered as the hand steering gear had been removed when the ship was converted. All the boats were shot up and rendered useless and the wireless aerial had carried away, the wireless set out of action. Many steam pipes were leaking and steam and hot water were issuing from unexpected places. The degaussing system which was then outboard had been rendered useless. The compasses were intact and the cliffs of Dover could be seen in the distance. A boat compass was taken down to the engine room platform and we proceeded in the direction of Dover steering by adjusting the speed of the screws. We arrived within about four or five miles off Dover harbour and were able to contact the destroyer HMS *Windsor* which came alongside and her surgeon boarded us together with a sick berth attendant with medical supplies and they immediately set to work on the seriously wounded cases, which we had been patching up as best we could, one grim scene having been enacted in the galley where the cook removed a soldier's leg.[3]

Astonishingly, in the later war years, *Mona's Isle* was reported to be haunted by the ghost of one of the soldiers killed on board during that crossing, which she made in tandem with the *King Orry*. Sergeant Dennis Cain of Douglas, who had been serving with the RAOC in France, had after four weeks of bombardment day and night made it to Dunkirk. He wrote to his uncle of this return journey:

I came home in the *King Orry* and in front of us was the *Mona's Isle*. She got badly knocked about, and there were a lot of men killed and wounded on her... He put a hole in her side about 4 feet and knocked her steering gear away. That was done from the air just outside Dunkirk. When we turned round on the *King Orry* he opened up with a shore battery on us from Calais. They were French 75s he had captured. He hit us a few times and killed and wounded some, but not as many as on the *Mona's Isle*. It was the speed of the *King Orry* and the way she was handled that got us out of it. She was also attacked from the air, but the planes were beaten off by the AA gun on the ship.[4]

However, *King Orry*'s second trip to Dunkirk was to be her last. There was now much more activity in the port as the evacuation was in full swing. As *King Orry* came into the harbour, she passed the still blazing destroyer HMS *Grenade*, which had been hit by a bomb earlier that day. One of *King Orry*'s officers, Sub Lieutenant Hayes, continues the story:

We were viciously bombed by the dreaded Stuka dive-bombers of the German air force. These aircraft emitted a shrill screaming whistle as they came straight down on your head. I later learned that these offputting screams were caused by mechanical sirens fitted to the undercarriage of the Stukas. About four bombers took part in our little drama. At least two bombs fell immediately ahead of the ship and didn't explode; two or three fell just clear of the stern, exploded and put the rudder out of commission. At least two more exploded close enough to the bow to blow small holes in the side of the ship both above and below the waterline. The noise was horrific and we were all petrified and momentarily stunned. The whole attack was over in seconds and we were left drifting helplessly in the harbour which was already cluttered with wrecks showing above the surface of the water.[5]

The *King Orry*'s engineer officer was her former Steam Packet chief engineer, now Lieutenant Laurence Quine, who was manning a bridge machine gun when the German dive-bombers came in and in his own words 'gave them some stick!' When the bombs landed either side of her, the blast blew him over the side into the water. Despite a lifetime at sea he could not swim, but luckily landed next to an abandoned life-raft and was saved. Hayes continues:

Our captain managed to manoeuvre the ship alongside the mole using the engines alone (no rudder...no steering). There was still a lot of enemy air activity in the area and we were ordered to abandon ship and get ashore. Unfortunately there didn't seem to be much safety in that course of action because we would have to transit a long, open and completely unprotected pier before we could reach any substantial cover. Most of the ship's company did get ashore, to the dock and huddled there hoping the bombers would not come back.[6]

Now urgent discussions took place regarding the extent of the damage. *King Orry* had no steering control beyond increasing or decreasing the power to her port and starboard propellers but at nightfall, with less risk of air attack, the decision was taken to at least try to get her away from the Mole. Hayes tells us:

When all was ready we slipped away from the pier, very gently, and proceeded to go astern slowly out through the narrow entrance...here we were, in the dark, going astern, with a wounded ship and a shaken crew – it certainly was not easy. The question in everyone's mind was would the captain turn the ship to port up toward the beaches and drive ashore there, as suggested by the embarkation officer, or would he turn to starboard, toward Dover and try for home? As we were slowly moving out of the harbour, the executive officer and I went around the upper deck and cut loose all the peacetime passenger benches that were in reality small life-rafts. They had been lashed down to special fixtures in the deck many years before to prevent movement in rough seas. Our remarkable executive officer had remembered the lashings and decided that now was the time they might be needed in their secondary role...while we were doing this, we noticed the ship's bow slowly turn to starboard – towards England. The 'old man' was going to go for it! Our joy was short-lived, however, because as she turned slowly, she also started to list heavily to starboard. At that point I decided that she was probably going to capsize, so I sprinted to my cabin which was on the upper deck to try to save some valuables.[7]

Hayes was able to step from the deck onto a raft and, as he later remarked, the most amazing thing was that he didn't even lose his hat. Another officer aboard *King Orry*, Lieutenant Jonathan Lee, remembered that a steward, in a state of shellshock and traumatized by the bombing, was patiently and meticulously sweeping up smashed glasses from the wardroom floor, even as the vessel was going down. Lee vividly remembered the water lapping nearer and nearer the bridge as she began to settle. As it finally engulfed the bridge he dived from the stern. Wreckage entangled the whistle lanyard, and as the *King Orry* disappeared beneath the water she let out a final moan as if it was her death cry.

By now the chartered vessels of the Steam Packet fleet were also heavily involved in the evacuation, and 29 May 1940 was to become the worst single day in the company's history for lives and tonnage lost. Alongside the *King Orry* as the Stukas attacked was the *Fenella*, one of the firm's newest and best vessels. She was

Third Engineer Reg Scarffe of HMS King Orry. He survived the sinking of the vessel at Dunkirk, but did not return to sea again. (Courtesy of Bernard Scarffe)

berthed at the Mole when she came under air attack, with bombs landing either side of her. One struck the Mole and blew concrete debris through her hull, sinking her where she lay. Robert Holmes of Douglas was a member of the crew of the *Fenella* along with his father-in-law, and wrote afterwards:

We sailed back and forth to Cherbourg, Le Havre, then set sail for Dunkirk. We were attacked by German planes [and] the *Fenella* was hit amidships; Roy Motion was on duty in the engine room at the time and had his leg fractured. We were told to abandon ship, so we all boarded the *Crested Eagle*...but halfway down the channel we were attacked by a Dornier who dropped two bombs on our stern. I remember being blown up the staircase in a sheet of flame but still had my wits about me, and looked about for father-in-law [but] I could not find him anywhere so I jumped into the water and was picked up by a destroyer's long boat, and taken back to its parent ship. I was landed at Margate hospital where my burns were treated. I spent two nights in Sea Breeze hospital then transferred to Orpington War Emergency Hospital.[8]

Among the other survivors of the *Fenella* were the Second Mate Westby Kissack, who later in the 1960s became a captain in the Steam Packet Company before being ordained, and Tom Helsby, the cabin boy from Liverpool who was wounded and picked up by the Germans, believed to be the only Steam Packet prisoner of war of the Second World War. A month or so later his parents received a letter from the chief officer of the *Fenella*, J.E. Quirk, who told them of the bombing of his ship and of the *Crested Eagle*. He wrote:

> It was just after this, that Tommy came to me & showed me where he had been burned on his face & hands by the explosion of the bomb, but he was soon bandaged up and said he felt alright...however the fire gained rapidly and Tommy asked me to lower him into the water – he had his lifebelt on and said that though he could not swim he would be able to float until he got out of the water...by this time there were hundreds of men in the water and boats trying to pick them up. He said he was alright, and I left him, as there were many more injured men who like Tommy asked to be lowered into the water.[9]

Quirk lost sight of him after this, but it transpired that Helsby had reached the beach and had been taken to a French hospital for treatment. The *Fenella* was to remain at her berth until the evacuation was over, the wreck finally being cleared by the Germans after the battle. In later years it was falsely rumoured that she had been refloated by the Germans, and then captured by the Russians at the end of the war. This was a result of a mix-up in the numbering system that the Germans had used to identify the wrecks in the harbour.

So bad did the bombing of ships at Dunkirk become that on 29 May Admiral Ramsay took the

Fourth Engineer R.R. Kermode of Laxey. He was sunk at Dunkirk first aboard the Fenella, *then the* Crested Eagle. *He made it to the beach in his vest and pants, having been in his cabin when the first bomb struck. He recalled in later years that the Red Cross would not help him as he was not a soldier. By a remarkable twist of fate he met his brother-in-law, an army ambulance driver, on the beach.*

decision to withdraw the eight most modern destroyers in the evacuation fleet; it was simply too risky to continue to expose them to danger. Three had already been sunk and six damaged. Nevertheless, the unarmed ships of the Merchant Navy were still expected to enter the inferno of Dunkirk. More loss of life was to follow on that dreadful day.

Mona's Queen was another modern ship commissioned by the Steam Packet Company in the 1930s. Launched five years before the war, she was a sleek and attractive vessel, especially in her white summer livery. She had been as popular with her crews as with the thousands of holidaymakers she brought to the island during the summer seasons. *Mona's Queen* had been engaged on a variety of other hazardous missions before being committed to the Dunkirk evacuation; she had picked up refugees from Rotterdam and Ostend and brought them back to England. Loaded with tons of explosives, she went next to Calais to land demolition squads to destroy the harbour. Finally she took troops out of Boulogne under German air attack. Her first trip to Dunkirk was under her regular master Radcliffe Duggan, known as 'the Rajah'. Shortly after the event he wrote an account of this first trip:

> When we were within two and a half miles of Dunkirk we were suddenly attacked and fired on by shore batteries... The first salvo went over our ship, the next one fell a little short, I thought the third would surely get us, so I ordered everyone to take what cover they could and lay down. In the meantime we had altered course to get out of range. The third salvo again fell short but splinters from bursting shells had badly damaged our degaussing line. One shell had penetrated the mainmast, then through two ventilators, hit a davit and scattered shrapnel all over the bridge, one piece having gone through a lifebuoy and then bedding itself in bridge timbers. We got out of gun range only to be attacked by two bombers whose aim luckily for us was poor. They in turn were shot down by one of our Spitfires, one hitting the water about fifty yards ahead of our ship...the dropping of bombs so near had damaged the steam pipes of the boiler; however, the chief engineer and second engineer worked like Trojans whilst we were in Dunkirk and made temporary repairs.[10]

He continued with a description of the bravery of some of his crew:

> [In Dunkirk] the Naval Officer in charge said he wished my signal man to send a message to a destroyer. My Radio Officer went up on top of the wheelhouse and sent the message without thinking of any danger from machine-gun bullets etc. A great bit of work...nor must I forget Boatswain Mr E. Watterson, he took over the steering whilst we were being bombed and shelled. He stood manfully at his task in a wheelhouse which was to a great extent composed of glass; he acted splendidly in getting troops on board at Dunkirk too. Mr Clucas too and Mr Studholm, 3rd officer worked untiringly. We left Dunkirk about ten o'clock that night.[11]

In fact Edgerton Watterson the bosun was to receive the Distinguished Service Medal for his bravery that day, and Ambler the radio officer received the Distinguished Service Cross. On her second trip to Dunkirk on 29 May 1940 *Mona's Queen* passed over a magnetic mine which she detonated. A series of remarkable and horrific photographs of this incident exist, which it is believed were taken from the destroyer HMS *Vanquisher*. One shows the cloud of steam that was released from the exploding boilers on *Mona's Queen*. Another shows the ship about to go down. A photograph of the survivors reveals the stress and fatigue from what they have been through, clearly visible on their faces. Many of the officers were not young men and the effect

The Distinguished Service Medal awarded to Bosun Edgerton Watterson of HM transport Mona's Queen *for bravery at Dunkirk. (Author's collection)*

Moments after Mona's Queen *struck a mine on the approach to Dunkirk, black smoke from the explosion can be seen mixing with lighter-coloured steam issuing from her ruptured boilers. (Imperial War Museum)*

of being suddenly plunged into cold water laced with diesel oil, amid the screams and shouts of the dying, can only be imagined.

The danger of magnetic mines was, however, well-known to the crew; her master had reported counting seventeen floating free in the supposedly safe channel as she approached Dunkirk harbour on her previous trip. It is widely believed that *Mona's Queen*'s degaussing equipment – a system of electric cables running around and underneath the ship and powered by the ship's generators, used to reduce its magnetic signature – had failed. Sometimes, when the crew switched generators, it was possible to forget to reconnect the degaussing system. More likely, however, is that the failure was caused by the damage sustained on the previous run. Tom Corteen of the *Manxman* reported many years later that his ship had passed over the same spot just before *Mona's Queen* and had not detonated the mine.

Whatever the cause, the ship's back was broken and she went down frighteningly fast. It is reported that it took less than two minutes for this to happen. Most of the engine-room crew

The badly-shaken survivors of Mona's Queen *in a lifeboat, shortly after she went down. (Imperial War Museum)*

were lost; the only engineer to survive from *Mona's Queen* was Lacey Knowles. The story reported at the time was that Bob Kneale, one of the other engineers, had been on deck and saw the devastation and flames of Dunkirk. He returned to the engine room and told Lacey that he should see the state of the town. Lacey had gone on deck to see for himself when the mine exploded. Consequently, he was the only one of the engine-room crew to survive. Of her complement of fifty-five, some twenty-four were lost that day.

There was great shock felt on the Isle of Man from the loss of these vessels and the sinking of the *Mona's Queen* in particular, given the speed with which she went down and the high death toll as a result. Many of the survivors lived with the memories of what had happened on 29 May for the rest of their lives. The Chief Officer Bob Clucas of Douglas carried a particular reminder of the loss of the *Mona's Queen*. Like other survivors he had little time to collect anything and all his personal effects were destroyed, including his Master's Certificate. This was effectively the tool of his trade – without it he could not do his

Chief Officer Bob Clucas, who lost all of his possessions including his Master's Certificate at Dunkirk. (Private collection)

job – so a replacement was issued by the Board of Trade, but it was endorsed with an official stamp to the effect that the original was lost at Dunkirk.

Other vessels from the Isle of Man Steam Packet Company carried on the evacuation, even in the knowledge of the loss of close friends aboard the ships that had been sunk. The *Lady of Mann* was another modern vessel built for the company in the 1930s. She was regarded as the flagship of the fleet, and carried out sterling work in the Dunkirk operations. *Tynwald* and *Lady of Mann* both carried far more troops than their Board of Trade official capacity allowed. Aboard the *Tynwald*, a number of crew members were decorated for making repeated crossings into the war zone. Among these were Donkeyman James Allan, Chief Officer Alan Watterson who was awarded the Distinguished Service Cross and one of the sailors, Tom Gribben, who was awarded the Distinguished Service Medal. The Radio Officer C.R. Mason was also awarded the Distinguished Service Cross. The purser aboard the *Tynwald* was William Lister, who was Mentioned in Dispatches, and who

Lacey Knowles (left), only survivor of the Mona's Queen *engine-room staff, in conversation with the father of one of the junior engineers, who was lost.*

later left a marvellous account of his own experiences in 1940. He reached *Tynwald* after returning from leave and boarded her just as she was about to set off for Dunkirk:

> I was busy paying the crew, I decided to pay out that night, I was that busy with the figures catching up, that I didn't look outside. Eventually I went out on deck, Lord bless my soul, it was like being in Hades, because there were fires everywhere, you could see the troops lining up along the beach, planes overhead, it was seven o'clock in the evening and that was my introduction to Dunkirk. Ships were virtually queuing up to go into the harbour. We didn't take them off the beaches, we had nothing to do with that, that had to be small craft. We went alongside the mole, the old wooden mole and there weren't any bollards, you just had to tie up as best you could. Next morning I went on my

second trip. While those poor devils were over there it was our bounden duty to go and get them. By this time though we were really saddened as the *Mona's Queen* had been sunk by a mine. The best thing though was not to think about it.[12]

Also aboard the *Tynwald* as a junior engineer was Harry Crawley. He wrote in 2008:

On the approach to Dunkirk we passed destroyers, naval trawlers, cross channel ships, including those of the Southern Railway, Great Western Railway and LNER, all of which were crowded with troops. Nearing Dunkirk we saw the town afire and the troops crowding the beaches. We berthed at the innermost berth of the jetty with shells bursting just short of us. The tide was low and it was not possible to get the gangways out, but luckily the ship possessed 14lb sledge hammers and we managed to break the concrete railings. We loaded troops and were overloaded according to the rules, but who worried about rules then.

Purser Bill Lister of SS Tynwald, *who was present with the ship at Dunkirk. (Courtesy of Junemary Moyle)*

On the next trip to Dunkirk we had to go into the harbour side of the jetty and we passed a trawler slowly sinking. We loaded French soldiers (they were some of the last to leave Dunkirk) and I will never forget Mr Tommy Cain on the jetty waving an iron rod and shouting '*Vite, vite*'; he was a great brave man, a DSC from World War One. This was my last run from Dunkirk and I was pretty stressed out, like the rest. The Chief Engineer had earlier become so stressed that he was unable to move and had to be led ashore by medics;

he was later replaced by Mr Tom Vickers who was 2nd Engineer on the *Viking*.[13]

On 30 May the evacuation was greatly aided by the weather: it was foggy and overcast which restricted enemy air activity, the Luftwaffe being grounded for much of the day. It was no coincidence that the largest single number of troops evacuated was taken out on this date; however, on 31 May the weather cleared again and losses from the Luftwaffe reached a peak on 1 June when thirty-one Allied ships were sunk by air attack. Thomas Cannell was a junior engineer aboard the *Ben-my-Chree*. He remembered:

> Friday 31st May we sailed to Dunkirk. Like so many days of the summer of 1940, it was beautifully sunny and calm. I had been in the dining saloon for dinner, so it was past mid-day when I came on deck, and found that we had already reached Dunkirk. A huge column of smoke was rising from the burning fuel tanks, but everything was so much quieter than I expected – somehow I had thought that there would be the continual sound of battle. We were standing off the harbour entrance – I suppose we were awaiting instructions to go alongside the Mole. A destroyer was standing quite near to us, and a naval rating was amusing himself by whistling in imitation of the sound of a falling bomb. We were to hear the real thing soon enough. We had approached Dunkirk from the west, and were moving very slowly and were close in. There were wrecks of ships all around, but closer inshore a sunken ship was sitting upright with much of her superstructure above water. We at once recognised her as the *King Orry*...
>
> The *Ben-my-Chree* slowly drifted past the harbour entrance, past the East Mole. There at the end berth on the outside of the East Mole lay the *Fenella*. At first glance, there seemed to be nothing wrong with her, except that there was no activity on the ship, and she seemed unusually low in the water. Then we realised she was sunk at her berth, and we wondered what had happened to her crew. Three ships lost out of the small Manx fleet on war service that we knew of – what about the other ships? The morale of the crew was badly shaken.[14]

It seems, however, that not every member of the crew was so perturbed by the situation. Second Lieutenant Frank Proudfoot of the Royal Artillery was among those who boarded the ship, exhausted and thirsty. He headed for the saloon, where he asked the Manx steward for whisky, perhaps to steady his nerves. The barman's laconic reply has gone down in folklore and convinced Proudfoot that with this kind of stoicism Britain could not possibly lose the war: 'Sir we are not allowed to open the bar whilst the ship is in port.'[15]

Nonetheless, the two days of intense bombing and air attack in Dunkirk had clearly affected others on the *Ben-my-Chree*. Today it is well known that every individual has a finite store of courage, and in repeated exposure to danger at some point a person's nerve will break. For some people this point will be reached sooner than others. Thomas Cannell continued:

> On a ship there is no place where one can take cover from bombing but it seemed to me that by staying on the main deck, with the top deck above me, the risk of being hit by bomb fragments was reduced. Perhaps there was another advantage in this – I couldn't see the bombers coming in to attack, but the explosions of the bombs sounded extremely close. So, during the afternoon the ship was gradually filling up with men. Some soldiers had filled their waterbottles with wine...but there seemed to be no hurry to get the ship away from the Mole and out to sea. In dangerous situations, one tries to rationalise the dangers, but there seemed to me to be an inexorable logic in that if the ship lay alongside the mole and was continually dive-bombed, eventually one bomb must score a direct hit. After all, we were a sitting duck, like an aunt sally at a fairground, not even a machine gun with which to fire back...the ship would be at least three hours taking troops aboard. In the boiler room that night, as the ship lay at Folkestone, I recall thinking to myself 'Surely they can't send us back into that Hell a second time!' But of course they did, and the next day we were crossing the Channel again to Dunkirk.[16]

Tom Corteen was aboard the *Manxman* (under her Captain P.B. Cowley) and his crew was similarly shaken:

In the evacuation of Dunkirk, I was both mate and second mate of the *Manxman* for the whole week. This was because the original mate had a nervous breakdown on the first run over to Dunkirk, so I had everything to see to and organise...some vessels would be in and out of Dunkirk in two or three hours if the troops were there in great numbers. So it was the actual time spent in the place that mattered, not the number of times in and out. The tension would ease every time one was leaving the place as it was in and around Dunkirk where all the action was taking place.

Another day we were on the point of leaving with a full load of troops after being alongside for about four hours, when some of the crew (who had been standing by to let go) came running to me in a very disturbed state. A destroyer had tied up alongside us and our troops were naturally swarming down on board her. She took nearly all of them, in fact she had to cast off or she would have been overwhelmed.

I told the destroyer commander what I thought about it all, the way he had upset my crew after what they had been through. They were in and out in minutes and we now had to wait alongside for hours again, awaiting troops who had to be rounded up and sent down the mole to us. No troops were left exposed on the mole unless there was a vessel alongside to receive them. This destroyer left us, the only vessel in, nothing even outside the pierheads. We were alone with no protection, not even a pop-gun, not a single tin hat amongst us, in fact, no soldier would even lend me his tin hat. When I had to go forward to pin the bow rudder whilst we were lying alongside, Hugh Crennell, the lamp trimmer (who had been a Lewis-gunner in the 1914–18 war) procured a Lewis gun and ammunition from one of the troops. I helped him to set it up, foreside of the bridge deck and also helped to load with practically all tracer bullets. He used that gun a few times before we got away. And he was certainly turning a few Stukas off course; I could see bullets passing right through the Stukas. I did not even realise that they were probably machine-gunning us as well. Without that gun, I am sure we would never have got out of Dunkirk, but Lamps had cracked up on the passage [back] and had to be put ashore.

I had not slept for a week; my nerves were keeping me going.[17]

Corteen was finally taken off the ship and replaced by a regular naval officer on the day the evacuation ended, 2 June 1940. At times since then, controversy has resurfaced in connection with the so-called 'mutinies' and refusals by crews of some Steam Packet vessels to sail to Dunkirk. However, little of what has been written is based on fact. It is necessary to examine the reactions and motives of some of the crews of the *Ben-my-Chree* and *Tynwald* in particular who have been tarred with this brush of mutiny, and to try to understand them. When requested by the Admiralty to make a third trip to Dunkirk, the master of the *Ben-my-Chree* Captain George Woods wrote back: 'I beg to state that after our experience in Dunkirk yesterday my answer is "No".'[18]

In fact the ship had already been damaged by bombing and there was every chance she would be hit again if she went back into Dunkirk without air cover. The master of the *Tynwald*, Captain Qualtrough, who was 63 years of age, sent back a similar reply, stating:

> Our crews have been continually on their feet all week and especially the deck officers who have had to be on their feet for so long. I myself have had 4 hours sleep for the week and am at present physically unfit for another trip like we have had... There are two more of the crew going ashore now absolutely nervous wrecks and certified by both the Army and Naval doctor.[19]

The crews had been extremely shaken, both by their own experiences and by the effect on morale of the loss of the *Mona's Queen*. Although the Royal Navy was still expecting the merchant ships to enter Dunkirk, it now considered the port too dangerous to risk its own destroyers there! It is also important to bear in mind that the refusals to return to Dunkirk were not confined to the Isle of Man Steam Packet Company (IoMSPCo). The master of the London North Eastern Railway (LNER) steamer *Malines* considered the risk to his ship so great and his crew so shaken, that without orders he left Dover and returned to his home port of Southampton. Several south-coast lifeboats also refused to return. The master of the Channel Islands ferry *St Helier* made a similar decision.

In the view of many, much more should have been done, both by the IoMSPCo. and the Admiralty, to provide relief crews so that the same men were not expected to make repeated trips without sleep or rest, though to be fair to the Steam Packet Company, they were short of experienced sailors. The word 'mutiny' is also iniquitous. Steam Packet Company minutes in the wake of Dunkirk make repeated references to 'refusals to volunteer'. This is a contradiction in terms: one can be asked to volunteer, but no blame should attach if one is not able for whatever reason to do so. As one member of the Merchant Navy stated: 'We suffered one of the highest casualty rates of the war, yet we were constantly being told by the authorities that we were civilians!' The word mutiny in the context of what happened at Dunkirk is inappropriate, if not to say inaccurate. If experienced Steam Packet captains and crews refused to sail, they would not have done so without good reason. All the crews had already undertaken at least one trip into Dunkirk and had experienced first-hand being a sitting-duck target without any air protection at all. Few born since can have any understanding of what this must have been like, though there is now a better awareness of post-traumatic stress. The campaign to pardon those shot for cowardice in the First World War has highlighted the fact that most people have a breaking-point if repeatedly subjected to mortal fear.

In 1940 neither the Admiralty in Dover nor the directors of the Steam Packet Company who were initially hostile towards the captains who had refused to sail had any real understanding of what their crews were being asked to do. To some extent the captains were damned if they did and damned if they didn't, for they were responsible for the safety of the ship which was company property, and it was for them to decide if the risk of damage was too great. Woods was censured by the company for leaving its property in the hands of strangers when the ship was temporarily taken over by the Royal Navy, but one has to ask what choice did he have? What efforts were made by the company to send a relief crew? Both Woods and Qualtrough were examined by Dr Charles Pantin at the behest of the company and both were diagnosed as having shellshock, yet the company declined to re-employ either of them after Dunkirk. In its defence, however, it did robustly rebuff Lord Granville's request to have the names of all those who had not gone back and to remove their pension rights.

I.O.M.S.P. Co. S.S. VIKING.   907.

The ageing SS Viking, *a ball of fire by night and a column of smoke by day. (Author's collection)*

Another aspect to bear in mind is that while the troops on the beaches were largely in their teens or early twenties, the men on the Steam Packet ships were often much older. The Steam Packet Company did not introduce a pension scheme until 1938 and it was not uncommon to find men sailing well into their sixties. Time and again when looking at crew members we find them in their fifties at Dunkirk. This is a significant factor: these were married men with families, and many of them had already been through the First World War. It has also been suggested in some quarters that those who did not wish to return to Dunkirk had political motives or were defeatist. This is unlikely, and the simplest answer is probably true: that all these men had been through an experience scarcely imaginable – some of them more than once – and they had simply had enough. Many had reached a point of physical and nervous exhaustion.

With the fall of France, the British Channel Islands only a few miles off the enemy-held coast became indefensible. Churchill conceded that they would have to be abandoned to the enemy, and they became the only British territory to be occupied by the Germans during the Second World War. Before that happened, however, an extraordinary evacuation took place. The people of Guernsey were offered the opportunity of escape for their children. Many reluctantly accepted it, and there were many tearful scenes as the Isle of Man Steam Packet vessel *Viking*, under her captain 'Ginger' Bridson, arrived to collect them. Bridson, from Castletown, was a veteran of the First World War and had worked his way up to the position of master after joining the company as a deck hand. He recalled that taking the children from their families was one of his hardest tasks. The *Viking* also had seen service in the First World War and was not in the first flush of youth. One of her Royal Navy escorts signalled to her: 'You are a column of smoke by day and a ball of fire by night. You are visible for miles.' Laconically, Bridson signalled back: 'We know!'[20]

In May 1940, with the threat of invasion following Dunkirk believed to be severe, Secretary of State for War Anthony Eden appealed for units of Local Defence Volunteers (later to be known as the Home Guard) to be formed across the British Isles. On the Isle of Man, within a few weeks 2,400 men had responded to the call and the force was organized into one artillery troop and two battalions of infantry. Arms for these volunteers were at first extremely scarce and were supplemented with shotguns, pikes and rubber truncheons; indeed, almost anything that could be pressed into service was used. There were appeals to the public for weapons and some firearms from the collection of the Manx Museum were actually handed over to the police in response to this. They were later returned to the museum when more modern equipment became available. In due course the Home Guard was to reach a high standard of efficiency. What they lacked in equipment, its members more than made up for in terms of local knowledge and high morale. They manned a total of fifty-two observation posts around the island from sunset to dawn, watching for a surprise attack from the air.

The Dunkirk evacuation was also quickly followed by the Battle of Britain. The RAF, which Air Marshal Dowding had held back during the defeat of France in anticipation of this moment, was now on the front line in the struggle with the Luftwaffe for control of the skies over Britain. One Manx airman who took part was Hubert

Flower of St Johns, who at 18 was the youngest airman to fly in the Battle of Britain. An air-gunner and wireless operator with 248 Squadron, he flew Bristol Blenheims. Although the Spitfire is most often associated with the battle, in fact many of these obsolete twin-engined machines were also in action and were usually outclassed by enemy Messerschmitts. In spite of the dire situation, morale in the RAF remained high. Edward Hughes, a son of Mrs Crellin of Fairfield House on Tynwald Street in Douglas, had joined the RAF in March 1939. At the time of the battle he had just been promoted to Aircraftsman 1st Class. Writing home, he stated that he could not understand men shirking joining up, because

> it will take every man Jack to win, and if all join it will be finished all the sooner. If they don't join, and we lose, we will all be killed and the shirkers will lose their jobs. I think it is up to every man to join and help to make this country fit for our children to live in.[21]

Obsolete biplane aircraft at RAF Ronaldsway, painted in 1940 by John H. Nicholson. (Courtesy of Manx National Heritage)

Other airmen were doing their bit on the Isle of Man. Ronaldsway airfield had been up and running for various airline services to a number of different parts of the United Kingdom since 1933. Upon the outbreak of war it had been designated as the assembly place for all the civilian aircraft in use in the British Isles, their crews being billeted at the Golf Links Hotel, Derbyhaven before the aircraft were dispersed on war work of various kinds. Although it had a small landing area and was often hampered by fog, nevertheless Ronaldsway was requisitioned by the RAF in June 1940 to allow No. 1 Ground Defence Gunners' School to move in. Trainees with machine guns on Fort Island, Derbyhaven would attempt to hit drogues towed by aircraft from Ronaldsway. The grass landing area was enlarged, but for the first half of the conflict target-towing aircraft consisted mainly of obsolete biplane types including Gloster Gauntlets, Hawker Harts and Westland Wallaces. Later known as No. 3 RAF Regiment School, this unit was to remain at Ronaldsway for nearly three years until it transferred to Hutton Cranswick in Yorkshire.

At the beginning of the Battle of Britain, in July 1940, the Chain Home Low (CHL) radar station at Cregneash (Meayll Hill) became operational, and would play a key part in victory. The previous year, Air Commodore Keith Park, Air Marshal Dowding's Senior Air Staff Officer had been delegated the job of siting the RAF's radar stations on the Isle of Man, as part of the Chain Home (CH) early warning system. Disregarding scientific advice to set up a single station on the summit of Snaefell, Park preferred the option of instead building two Chain Home facilities, one at the north end of the island and the other to the south. The sites selected early in 1940 were at Bride to the north and Scarlett to the south. Both facilities were designated Advance Chain Home (ACH) installations, being brought on line with temporary shorter timber masts to support the transmitter arrays, pending the availability of standard 'west coast' 325ft guyed steel masts. However, neither station would be in use until September 1940.

Developed at the same time as the CH system, CHL stations were able to detect low-flying aircraft that could not be picked up by the other network and were intended to fill the gaps left in it. Because radio waves do not follow the curvature of the earth, a potentially hostile plane flying low enough over the sea could avoid

A generic sketch of a Chain Home Low radar station. The 'mattress-style' antenna is clearly visible. (R.J.C. Thomas)

detection until it was too late. However, it was found that high-frequency radar equipment with a wave length of 1.5 metres could give cover against low-flying aircraft and this equipment also did not require the huge mast necessary for use with CH. Instead it used a mattress-type aerial which could be rotated. There were two CHL facilities proposed for the island. To the south, Cregneash CHL station was built on top of Meayll Hill; this initially supported the CH station at Scarlett and subsequently that at Dalby. A CHL base at Maughold in the north was selected to work with the CH station at Bride, though it was later abandoned. The early CH sites along Britain's east coast had faced Germany, but the fall of France left Britain's west coast vulnerable to attacks from aircraft flying from French bases over the Irish Sea. This in turn proved the wisdom of developing a west coast network, and the Isle of Man's Chain Home stations provided air cover for much of north-west England by reporting to the RAF's 9 Group filter room at Longley Lane, Preston.

The Royal Navy was also interested in radar as a means of detecting submarines and surface targets. Admiral Somerville, Commander-in-Chief Western Approaches, had initially earmarked the Calf of Man as a location for a radar station to protect Liverpool bay; however, his staff suggested that they confer with the RAF about their intentions and the result was that the naval station was incorporated into the Cregneash site. Thus Meayll Hill became an important facility, initially equipped with two AMES Type 2 radars. These were later supplemented with an AMES Type 31, Coastal Defence (CD) No.1 MkV system (manned by WRENs and used by the navy to monitor shipping) and also AMES Type 52 equipment. It was a key surveillance station, monitoring the primary shipping lanes from North America to Liverpool. There was no accommodation on site, and several houses on the road from Port Erin were used as billets for female service personnel from the WAAF and WRENs. Male personnel were accommodated in the Golf Links Hotel in Port St Mary. Meals were normally eaten at the billets but those on duty had to eat at the station. As

there was no running water on site, fresh water had to be carried up by the RAF vehicles transporting the changes of 'watch' personnel. Extra rations of milk, eggs and butter were also obtained from Church Farm in Cregneash village. Today little remains to be seen at Meayll Hill, although two pill-boxes that guarded the site and the bases of a number of buildings can be easily identified.

Although RAF Jurby had been planned as a training station and its first unit was No. 5 Air Observers' School, life here was not all about practice. Some active fighter squadrons arrived at Jurby in the autumn of 1940, starting with the Boulton Paul Defiants of 307 Squadron. These turret-armed fighters were followed by three Hawker Hurricane squadrons (258, 302 and 312) and later the Supermarine Spitfires of 457 Squadron for convoy patrol sorties,

Kurt Schwitters, the avant garde German artist who fled from the Nazis before the war. He was interned in Hutchinson Camp, where he made abstract collages and sculptures from porridge. (Author's collection)

which were highly important duties. However, the most distinctive feature of the island from 1940 onwards was its internment camps for enemy aliens and political detainees, established in rows of hotels and boarding houses in Douglas, Onchan, Peel, Ramsey and in the south in Rushen. Each had a slightly different atmosphere; Hutchinson Camp in Douglas, for example, contained large numbers of exiled artists and intellectuals and gained a reputation as the 'university' of the Isle of Man.

While these internment camps were for single male internees, that which was established in the south of the island in Port Erin and Port St Mary (known as Rushen Camp) was for women and children and later for married couples. This camp is believed to have been unique in this respect, having no parallel in any other part of the world during the war. It was also unusual in that, unlike other camps, the residents were not evicted from their premises, but had women and children billeted with them. The camp was established by the Manx authorities and Government Secretary Bertram Sargeaunt described it in a letter to MI5, which had requested details of the arrangements:

> We commenced to erect a barbed-wire fence across the peninsula, and to close all roads except the main road, where a police guard is stationed day and night, and the traffic in and out of the enclosure thereby regulated.
>
> You will appreciate that within the enclosure there are also living some 3,000 Manx residents, and these must necessarily be allowed freedom of movement out of and into the enclosure in order that they can conduct their normal business. Many of them for instance come into Douglas daily for business purposes. All these local people are of course known to the police, and they are allowed to pass in and out on presentation of their National Registration Identity Cards, which in the case of Manx people have special letters.[22]

No one who lived outside the camp area was permitted to enter except for business reasons, and they would not be admitted simply for leisure purposes such as going to the cinema or bathing in the sea. The internees, however, were allowed freedom of movement within the enclosure and were permitted to undertake these and

Female internees at Kennilworth Guest House, inside the Rushen Internment Camp. (Courtesy of Cathy Clucas)

other leisure activities such as playing tennis. While some women and children adjusted well to internment, tensions arose in the camp through the mixture of Jewish refugees and Nazi loyalists. The Manx authorities had had neither the time nor the awareness of the necessity to segregate them as the camp was being established. One internee, Erna Nelki, wrote:

> The choice of allocation was arbitrary; we had to share a house, a room and very often a double bed with a complete stranger... We were amazed at our accommodation, as we had expected barracks... The quality of accommodation varied... Our house with twenty women had only one bathroom but there was a water jug and basin in every bedroom. The first few weeks were very anxious and demanding ones. Despair, unhappiness and insecurity dominated. There was only one Commandant's Office and three thousand women, and there were queues, pushing, shoving, talking, flying rumours, crying and increased hysteria. These first few weeks stand out like a horrible dream in our memories.[23]

The camp commandant, Dame Joanna Cruikshank, is a somewhat controversial figure. From a military background and something of an authoritarian, it has been claimed that she found more in common with the Nazi women than the Jewish refugees. It is clear, however, that she faced a herculean task in establishing a camp from scratch in a short space of time, as the inmates were actually arriving. The restrictions imposed on the Manx population by the camp, in particular the difficulties that some local servicemen found in getting to their homes while on leave, caused a degree of tension and friction, but the initial fears that certain families had about having Germans billeted on them soon melted away (indeed, some lasting friendships were formed). The economic importance of the Women's and Married Camps to the boarding-house-keepers of the southern towns was also quickly appreciated. Aside from the considerable number of school-age children in the camp (estimated at 350), a number of babies were born to interned mothers in the camp during the war. Another unique aspect was the service exchange scheme set up by Dr Ruth Borchard, by which women exchanged work for credits or other goods. A form of currency was used, made from the cardboard of cereal boxes.

Another slightly unusual camp was Parkfield, a large private house on the outskirts of Douglas, which for a brief period held senior Nazis and German diplomats, including the German ambassador to Iceland. They were closely guarded until, some while later, they were exchanged for the British ambassador to Holland and his entourage and left for Germany via neutral Portugal.

With the entry of Italy into the war on Germany's side in June 1940, Italians living in Britain were also now considered to be enemy aliens and were arrested by the police. Among them was Charles Forte, the London-based hotel and catering entrepreneur who would go on to found the Trusthouse Forte group. After being assembled at Kempton Park racecourse, his group was shipped to the Isle of Man and sent to the Palace Camp on Douglas sea front, where at that time he recalled that there were more than 3,000 Italians from all over the British Isles. Although they were captives, he records that they were never pushed around or ill-treated in any way by the guards. The worst aspect for Forte was being away from his mother and family when they really needed him, when the blitz

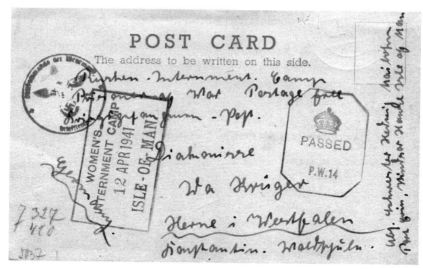

This postcard from a female internee at Windsor House, Port Erin carries censor stamps both from the Manx camp and the swastika and eagle of the Nazi authorities. (Author's collection)

on London started in September 1940. He wrote of his stay in the Palace Camp:

> The worst part of the initial period was sitting around with nothing to do but play cards and talk. This did not last long, however. As I spoke better English than most, the camp commandant, Captain Myers, asked me to become the liaison between the internees and the camp command. I was given an office and an assistant and soon became very busy. One of my jobs was to write petitions to the Home Office on the internees' behalf, to vet their applications and help them write their letters. Of course everybody was petitioning the Home Office – including me. I stated my own case very forcibly, but after a few weeks I gave up any hope of being released.
>
> I acquired a degree of minor importance in the camp and was allowed in and out of the palisade to walk across to the commandant's office without an escort. It gave me a certain sense of freedom and dignity. To an extent the work reconciled me to the miserable circumstances I was in. I

began to feel less bitter and more philosophical. Perhaps after all I was comparatively fortunate: in the Western Desert, in the air, and on the sea thousands of men were suffering and dying. I made myself accept that internment was my part in the war.

One day Captain Myers said to me: 'There are some fascists in there, aren't there, Forte?'

'Where?'

'In the camp. Who are they?'

'Look, Captain Myers,' I said, 'first of all there aren't any fascists. They are all people like me. They have no interest in politics and if they had, do you want to treat me as a spy or as a man who is helping you do this work? You don't think I would tell you, do you?'

'I don't know.'

I looked him straight in the eye. 'Well I know.'

He gave me an odd look, whether of approval or disapproval I do not know. I was convinced the conversation would lose me my job – the only thing that made the camp bearable.[24]

He was wrong, however. His sense of integrity did not cost him his job, but shortly afterwards his appeals to the Home Office were successful and he was released. Not every hotel on Douglas sea front contained internees. Terry Cringle, whose parents ran Studley House on Queen's Promenade, remembered:

My family's boarding house block was not taken over. We were allowed to stay there, and we were used as barracks for the soldiers, for the guards, which was a very exciting time for a young man, to have a house full of men in khaki and with rifles, SMLE .303 Short Lee Enfields, and bayonets, and all this kit, and it gave me an immense interest in soldiering.[25]

A large number of such soldiers was necessary to man these camps, and at its peak the total of guards reached about 1,500. In order to oversee these and other troops in training, in July 1940 Western Command had decided to establish an Isle of Man Garrison Headquarters, which was housed at Marathon, the former home of the late Mr Samuel Harris, High Bailiff of Douglas. Soon the building was a hive of industry with typists, wireless-operators and a considerable number of troops. There was also a teleprinter keeping it in direct communication with the UK.

The first OC was Brigadier Swinton. After he left, his place was taken by Brigadier G.N. Ford, CB, DSO. At that time there was good reason to fear for the security of the island, which it was anticipated would be invaded, and the 14th Battalion, King's Regiment was sent to strengthen the garrison. With the Home Guard and 166th Officer Cadet Training Unit (OCTU), the island soon appeared to be a great military camp. Next there came the 30th Cheshires under Lieutenant Colonel Hazelhurst, transferred

Methodist minister J.T. Passant of Ramsey. He was a pacifist and gave advice and encouragement to a number of local conscientious objectors before leaving the island in August 1940.

from his post as adjutant to the King's. They took over the defence of Laxey and Castletown. The Cheshires, which included many Manxmen, left later for garrison duty in North Africa. Then came the Royal Corps of Signals under Lieutenant Colonel Lane, and later an RAF regiment who had their camp in the large boarding-houses on the front near the Castle Mona Hotel.

Another man of integrity and intense personal conviction in Douglas was Norman Cretney. A well-known Methodist local preacher and Sunday school worker, in August 1940 he was unconditionally registered as a conscientious objector by the local tribunal. He was subjected to a gruelling cross-examination, but maintained that his attitude was based on the will of God. His brother, who was due to be called up the following week, testified to the sincerity of Cretney's beliefs, and was complimented on his evidence by the members of the tribunal. In his application to be registered as a conscientious objector, Cretney had stated:

As a Christian, I recognise the claim of every person to interpret their own sense of God's will for them in every sphere of activity, including service to nation and to the world. This right has been acknowledged by the British Houses of Parliament and the Insular Legislature, these assemblies having thus assented to the principle that every individual citizen has the right to avail himself of this freedom of conscience, provided that it is a sincere conviction. I submit that my whole life for the past few years and my record of service has witnessed to the sincerity of my religious feelings. I have been a pacifist for six years and a member of the Methodist Peace Fellowship since 16th June, 1937. In a very real way I am deeply conscious of the very distressing circumstances of the present hour, and have prayerfully and thoughtfully reconsidered my position in the light of recent events, but I dare not depart from the principle that my first duty is to obey the direction of the Will of God as this is interpreted for me – prayer and communion with Him. I recognise the increasing demands of Humanity upon one who professes to be a Christian in these days, but humbly suggest that as God has been gracious enough to use my labours in preaching and leadership amongst young people that this is the service to which He has called me, and in following this rule I believe this is the highest form of service I can do, both for the nation and the world. I humbly and sincerely make this claim to be placed unreservedly on the register of Conscientious Objectors in the Isle of Man, being certain that the justice and fairmindedness of my fellowmen will acknowledge my absolute sincerity in this matter. In conclusion, I submit that 'Here I stand; I can do no other.' So help me God.[26]

It is interesting to observe that a particularly Manx strand of pacifist Methodism linked many of the objectors of the Second World War with those of the first. The contrast between the treatment of conscientious objectors from the First and Second World Wars, however, was striking. Intense patriotic feeling in the first war had made them reviled, almost hate figures. Now their stance was usually respected, and rather than prison sentences they were generally given the chance to do good work in their

Members of Kirk Michael Auxiliary Fire Service around 1940. Note the mix of civilian and fire service attire. (Courtesy of Kirk Michael Fire Station via Barry Bridson)

communities. Some joined the Auxiliary Fire Service, which at this time was undergoing rapid expansion with 20,000ft of hose being purchased as well as additional appliances including 100 stirrup pumps and 300 uniforms for its members.

As the summer of 1940 gave way to autumn, the Luftwaffe turned its attention away from RAF airfields and began the systematic night bombing of British cities. In Manchester, some fine work in fighting fires was done by a Manxman, John Mylroie Kelly of Foxdale, who was second officer in the Stretford and Urmston Fire Brigade. He received the British Empire Medal for his courage and leadership in tackling a blaze at a gas holder. Ports such as Liverpool were particularly heavily bombed, not just because they were strategically important but also because in a blackout they could be found simply by following the coastline. Following the blitz on Liverpool, policemen from that district were sent to the Isle of Man for rest and recuperation. A number of Liverpool children were also reported to have been evacuated to the island, but exact numbers are not clear. Certainly it is true that many of the boarding-houses were owned by Liverpool or Lancashire families, so it would not be uncommon for a child

Princesses Elizabeth and Margaret. Did they spend time on the Isle of Man during the blitz on London? (Author's collection)

from the industrial cities of the north to be sent to stay with an aunt or uncle living in Douglas. There were also rumours that the Princesses Elizabeth and Margaret had come to the Isle of Man in secret to avoid the blitz on London. There is circumstantial evidence to support this theory because the wife of the Lieutenant Governor, Lord Granville, was the Queen's sister. It is believed that the princesses may have stayed at Ballamanaugh, Sulby, home of Sir Mark Collett. Collett was possibly the wealthiest man on the island, and both his father and nephew became governor of the Bank of England.

By the autumn of 1940, shortages and hardship were already becoming notable among those who had relied upon tourism as a means of making their living, with the *Isle of Man Times* reporting:

> A contract has been let by the Northern Water Board for the construction of a reservoir at Blockeary, Sulby, and jobs for sixty men may be filled up in the days ahead. Some weeks ago the Highway Board commenced work on the Sulby river, under the terms of the Land Drainage Acts. But it is considered that river work is not suitable for the

winter. There are good chances of private employment but the men taken on will need to be able-bodied. The majority of men for whom the Government is now asked to provide are not the kind whom a contractor would accept if he could possibly get better. Men of good physique and experience have taken jobs across the water. Some of those employed on river-cleaning have been boarding-house-keepers – which doesn't mean that they are an inferior type of humanity, but does mean that they are unaccustomed to heavy manual labour.[27]

Many men who were facing hardship, the report continued, looked enviously upon the internees being employed on farms around Ramsey. The farmers, for their part, claimed that labour was hard to find, and the internees of course were cheap at only a shilling a day. Even the Board of Agriculture used internee labour, and did so while exercising their new powers to take land for food production. They drained and cleared land at Glenlough, Marown (adjoining part of the newly-cleared and widened River Dhoo) and proposed to plant it with vegetables. They considered that using internees was the only way in which the work would be economic.

As well as foodstuffs, restrictions on imports also affected fuel, as all the coal consumed on the Isle of Man had to be shipped in. As the weather grew colder, RAF trainees billeted at Bridge House in Castletown could not resist the temptation to break in to the adjoining boathouse in search of firewood. Here they encountered the *Peggy*, the eighteenth-century yacht built by local gentleman George Quayle, which was entombed in her boat cellar. It is said that the trainees began by burning the ship's deck planks as fuel, and the story has it that they would have burned the rest of the historic vessel as well had they not been posted away overseas in the nick of time. One fact is certainly true: the recruits found a considerable quantity of unissued eighteenth-century notes from Quayle's bank in the house and many kept them as souvenirs. A number were returned to the island by ex-RAF personnel in later years.

It was in the matter of food, however, that shortages were perhaps most keenly felt. Housewives were encouraged to use margarine over butter, as the authorities felt this was more easily sourced. Other substitute food items were less palatable. One cookery expert writing in the *Ramsey Courier* that Christmas advised:

Almost all the ingredients for a Christmas pudding now cost more, and there is the added difficulty of how to squeeze enough out of the sugar and fat ration to make it. Even the unrationed ingredients present a problem. Eggs, for instance. They are scarce and dear, and, in some districts, almost unobtainable. Domestic science people appreciate this question of cost and scarcity. So I have asked one of them – a professional cookery expert – to prepare a recipe specially with an eye to economy and wartime food shortages. The pudding requires the minimum of fat, no sugar or eggs; and whereas it is not nearly so rich as the conventional recipe, it is quite good. To make the pudding a darker brown, mix a teaspoonful of gravy browning – the unflavoured variety of course – to the milk. This pudding should be eaten right away, and not be put by to mature, as with peacetime mixtures.[28]

A list of ingredients followed, but bilious (in both senses) regular correspondent John Crellin of Lezayre was less than impressed and suggested the following week that mixing them might well

provide an impression of the chaos in the Italian armies on the approach of the Greek troops. And as a meeting with the pudding on one's table might be almost as deadly, it might be well to include at least one medico (who doesn't take plum pudding) amongst one's guests this Christmas.[29]

Thus the end of 1940 found the Isle of Man home to great numbers of visitors, both friendly and hostile. These included the thousands of military personnel billeted on the island, and also the numerous inhabitants of the internment camps, some of whom expressed pro-Axis views but many of whom did not. If 1940 had been an apprehensive time for the average Briton with invasion only narrowly (and for the time being) averted, how much worse must it have been for those refugees from Nazi tyranny, perhaps anxious for news of loved ones, and now conveniently corralled in camps on the Isle of Man ready for their oppressors to find, should Britain fall?

A home-made Chanukkah card from a Jewish internee in Mooragh Camp, Ramsey. December 1940. (Author's collection)

CHAPTER THREE

1941: IOM Go To It!

The year 1941 was perhaps the hardest of the war for Great Britain. With France defeated and the United States not yet a combatant, for the first six months she would fight on alone, with only the support of her Empire and colonies (valuable though that was). Although Hitler's attack on the Soviet Union in the summer served to distract German attention away from mainland Britain, the parlous state of the Red Army at this time meant that the Russians were able to offer little in terms of practical help; indeed, what few items Britain could spare in terms of arms and supplies were being sent east to try to keep the USSR in the war. In the North African and Mediterranean theatres, Britain would continue to fight the Germans and Italians for control of the strategically-vital Suez Canal and the approaches to it.

On the island, by January 1941 after more than a year of conflict, the economic position had greatly deteriorated owing to war conditions. Many of its people were passing through a time of anxiety, and indeed in some cases of great distress. As an illustration of the shortage of often the most basic commodities, in the spring of that year the steamer *Madge Wildfire* ran aground at Langness. She was carrying a quantity both of Lux soap bars and of soap flakes for washing clothes. These were in such short supply that a good deal of pilfering from the wreck occurred. In an odd foreshadowing of the plot of the famous film *Whisky Galore*, the police became involved, houses were searched and several well-known and respected people were charged with looting. In another incident, a ship carrying thousands of cigarettes ran aground. Enterprising smokers were sometimes to be found afterwards, carefully drying out tobacco on the tops of stoves and ranges.

The visiting industry had suffered considerably, and the plight of those engaged in the catering trade was a sorry one. It was only thanks to the many internment camps and similar establishments organized locally that things were not worse. Other income came from billeting and the requisitioning on a hire basis of numbers of properties. Unlike the situation in the Great War, it had proved impossible to set up any significant or lasting war industries on the island. Mr Cubbon, chairman of the Isle of Man Bank, told shareholders in January:

> As regards agriculture it is safe to say that the war has brought about a higher and perhaps a reasonably profitable level of prices. Restrictions have been imposed, and restrictions always are irksome, but so far it would seem that a fair price standard has been maintained as between producer and consumer. Farmers are called upon to cultivate to the utmost of their capacity, and to do so is of vital importance, as I am sure they realise. It has to be acknowledged that the road is not an easy one to travel, and the drift from the land, which so regrettably has gone on for many years has added to the present-day problem. Let us hope that ways and means will be found and that the island will be able to contribute its full share of the food requirements which are essential to that victory and peace to which we look forward so eagerly.[1]

Mr T.H. Cowin complimented the chairman on the splendid position of the bank, and observed that tradespeople were largely dependent on the prosperity of agriculture. As president of the Agricultural Society, he hoped the Manx government would give the farmers a fair chance by raising prices to the English level. As well as income from the British government for the upkeep of the internment camps, the island also benefited from the host of training facilities that had sprung up at various places. A good example was No. 166 OCTU, now stationed in the Villiers hotel on the Douglas promenade. One of its cadets, named Edward Winter Anstey, was to have long and distinguished military service, but his diary recounts the early days of his career in training on the Isle of Man:

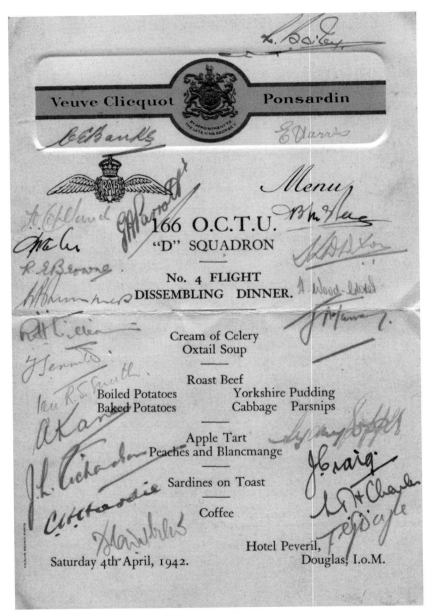

A menu from a 166 OCTU dinner held at the Peveril Hotel, Douglas. The unit trained both army and RAF officer cadets. (Author's collection)

Thursday 3rd April 1941:

Things taken easily in anticipation of the '24 hour scheme' traditional last & highest hurdle of the 166 OCTU. Commenced at 1715hrs. Weather excellent. Overcast but not heavy. We enjoyed this first phase, a sound 9-mile route march done at a smart pace and with few hitches. This brought us to the famous barn at Ellerslie and we bedded down amongst sacks of potatoes and bales of straw. Cocoa and biscuits were there under the chaperonage of Lynham, CSM & HQ staff who hereafter turned up in strength on odd occasions with containers of food from Douglas. Lynham hereby became an even more welcome addition to the scenery than he usually is. Unreservedly I name him a grand fellow.

Friday 4th April 1941:

Slept more soundly than anybody until roused at 0300 hrs. Feet were cold on rising so should have spent a restless dawn anyway. Hot tea awaited us and the second phase was rapidly under way. Commenced with a difficult march in pitch darkness up to the forward edge of Archallagan Plantation & there 13 Platoon crossed a flooded meadow on assault boats. The customary difficulties of the operation were in no way mitigated on this occasion and after being soaked above the ankles in the preliminary operations I got out & pushed the thing across. Then followed a tedious spell on the far bank to cover kapok bridging by the remainder of the company. The dawn broke even more cold & grey than it usually is & our own soaked limbs needed constant exercise to keep off actual numbness. All bad things come to an end however and we had a brisk march down to the village school at Foxdale where a sketchy breakfast was partaken. 3rd phase saw me commanding the company in defence which went fairly well though Whyte commanding the left platoon overran his boundaries and tried to form a battalion front. The final phase, the attack on Garey, developed about 1100 under Jim Loveridge. This action, by far the most difficult we had done, was fought when we had begun to feel the strain and was not decisively successful. Control became the worst problem and Corbett, who was o/c 13 [Platoon], fought much on his own without superior orders. I found this quite a tough spell.[2]

In spite of the hard physical nature of exercises such as this, there was still time for a social life and Anstey had found himself a regular female companion for visits to the cinema and other entertainments in Douglas. When the twenty-four-hour scheme brought his training to a successful conclusion, it was with stiff upper lips that the two agreed to part company forever on their final night together. However, in his diary he notes that so mixed were his feelings on leaving Douglas later that month that he could not for long remain on deck alone with his thoughts, preferring instead the rowdy atmosphere of the ship's bar where his comrades were lustily singing *She'll Be Coming Round The Mountain*.

Anstey's service would soon take him to the Middle East, at that time the only active theatre of operations for the British army. Also in this arena was the Manx Regiment, now stationed in Egypt, mainly on airfield defence. In the early part of the year, 129 Battery had been detached from the regiment and sent to

A 37mm Bofors gun of the Manx Regiment on airfield defence in Egypt, early 1941. (Courtesy of the Manx Aviation Preservation Society/Manx Regiment Museum)

Crete, where defences were being strengthened against a possible Axis attack. Following the fall of Greece, Hitler saw the island as a useful stepping-stone for further advances, while Churchill wanted to turn it into another Malta, a thorn in the Axis side in the Eastern Mediterranean. For the first few months their stay on the island had a holiday feel. The locals were friendly and the ack-ack gunners patronized the Cretan cafés which sold cheap wines and spirits as well as expensive Australian beer. With the arrival of British warships in Suda Bay, German air attacks on the island grew in intensity, and on 20 May 1941 the sight of many hundreds of different coloured parachutes in the sky signalled the beginning of an airborne assault and the battle for Crete. One of the Manx Regiment gunners, David Gray, remembered:

> We soon realised our biggest disadvantage was that we were static. Although we had been trained in our early days as a mobile battery, we had been supplied on arrival in Crete with static guns. In fact, our first job was to install these guns in pads of reinforced concrete three feet thick, so we had to stay put.[3]

Paratroopers fall from the sky during the German attack on Crete, May 1941. One aircraft has been hit by anti-aircraft fire. (Author's collection)

They were forced to try to camouflage the bright brasswork of the guns with bootblack, and poured used engine oil onto the gleaming white pebbled floor of the gunpit in order to make it less conspicuous. Even though the Manx gunners scored numerous hits on the Stukas and Messerschmitts overhead, the Germans managed to capture the airfield at Maleme and after that they could pour troops in by transport plane. Crete quickly fell. Another Manx Regiment gunner present here was John Stevenson. When the situation on the island became untenable, he and some comrades were ordered to make their way south for evacuation:

> We walked most of the 40 miles over the mountains to Sphakia and we had to hide in caves during the day because the Germans were back and forward with their fighter planes looking for us, strafing and bombing and whatever. Each night we had to await the Navy coming in to take us off and we were actually on the water's edge when the Colonel came along and said, 'I'm sorry gentlemen, they're not taking any more off and tomorrow we'll be surrendering to the Germans', so that was it.[4]

Back on the Isle of Man, great shock was felt over the loss of Crete. On one level, the newspapers were filled for day after day with photos of those who were missing, and hardly anyone would not have known at least one family affected. On another, however, the battle had showed just how easily an island could be captured from the air if parachute troops could secure an airfield, underlining the extreme importance of defending Ronaldsway and Jurby. Overall, the conditions for the Manx prisoners now in German hands contrasted sharply with those of their opposite numbers in British camps.

David Gray recalled that he and his fellow prisoners subsisted on German coffee for breakfast, no lunch and a bowl of vegetable soup in the evening. At one point, being a butcher by trade, he was able to get a job in a German meat-processing factory which had the advantage that he was sometimes able to steal sausages. In contrast, those on the Isle of Man were both better fed and treated with a leniency which many locals felt bordered upon kid gloves. In the spring of 1941 a member of the British Union of Fascists, John Charnley, was sent to the Isle of Man to be detained under Defence of the Realm Regulation 18b. This covered anyone who was felt to be a threat to national security. His destination, Peveril Camp on Peel promenade, contained a mixed bag of inmates of various political persuasions and outlooks. He remembered as well as British Union members there were members of the Link and the Anglo-German Fellowship, as well as IRA members and men of other nationalities who had been arrested on the direct recommendation of MI5 and MI6. Among the more notable inmates in the camp were Quentin Joyce, younger brother of William (Lord Haw-Haw); Professor Darwin-Fox; Harry St John Philby (father of the traitor

Gunner Tommy Morrissey, Manx Regiment, captured on Crete in 1941. (Courtesy of the Quirk family)

Kim Philby); Squadron Leader Frederick Rutland of Jutland fame; and Admiral Niki Wolkoff of the Imperial Russian Navy.

Charnley was designated as a cook, and when two IRA men and a BUF member were recaptured after two days on the run, he prepared a meal for them and requested an escort of guards to take him to the guardroom where the men were being held. After a phone call to administrative headquarters, permission was refused. Undeterred, Charnley tried again, this time accompanied by the camp leader Mick Clarke (the former BUF councillor for Bethnal Green). He continues:

> The reply came back that the decision had been made by the Acting Commandant, who had decided that since the escapees had been without a hot meal for over two days it would not harm them to go without for three days. At this I 'blew my top', and stormed away from the gate in a very angry frame of mind.
>
> [His] action provoked a spontaneous outburst of resentment, which resulted in a demonstration at the

A group from the British Union of Fascists, detained at Peveril Camp in 1941 under Section 18B of the Defence of the Realm Act. (Friends of Oswald Mosley)

main gate demanding a change of heart. [The Acting Commandant] remained adamant, and as a result a full-scale riot developed, involving practically the whole camp, and forcing the retreat of the guards from the main gate under a hail of missiles. It was probably my justifiable anger which sparked off the riotous assembly which followed, since my telling of the circumstances lost nothing in the recounting of the story.

Outside the perimeter was the Creg Malin Hotel, a fairly large building with outhouses. The hotel was the administrative offices for the military and its outhouses were used for minor administrative purposes and included a large room for visitors.

Whenever the military attempted to enter the camp in a bid to restore order, they were met with a hail of missiles. The garden walls of the lower houses were torn down and hurled against the main gate and the hotel itself, most of whose windows abutting the side road were smashed as a result.

The riot lasted throughout the night... Appeals by the military for a cessation of hostilities were met with the demand that I should be allowed to take a meal to the guardhouse, but [the Acting Commandant] consistently refused to give way. So did we. Eventually reporters arrived and were provided with seats at the upper window of the hotel. We countered with jets of water from fire hoses attached to the house taps abutting the road. Many press men were thoroughly drenched to our great delight, for they were no friends of ours.[5]

Shortly after the riot, *Isle of Man Times* cartoonist Dusty Miller published a sketch entitled *Peel the Gloves Off*, which showed impotent guards and Peel commissioners pleading with the Home Office for more powers, while in the background a caricature of a fascist thug laughed at them. However, one outcome of the riot was that the army was withdrawn from camp administration, which was now taken over by the Metropolitan Police, and confined simply to guarding the camp perimeter.

Another detainee held there around this time was Hector Emmanuelli, a Briton of Italian descent. He had been in Italy improving his language skills when war with Germany had broken out and had returned to England shortly afterwards. The authorities were suspicious of his motives, and so he was arrested and detained as a British fascist sympathizer rather than interned as an Italian enemy alien. He had fond memories of his time in Peel and wrote:

Cartoonist Dusty Miller. The Fascists held at Peel were often targets of his wartime cartoons. (Courtesy of Helen and Jack Cain)

The detainees organised various activities, including football and boxing matches, lectures and language classes. They also swapped books and ran a drama group. People read a lot and took part in discussion groups. Some wrote poetry and painted. Of all the camps, Camp 'M' was the most civilised I had been in, and its inmates were treated humanely. It was in a way almost like a mini-university. I certainly learnt a lot there. The thought of my brother Louis, who was exposed to the very real dangers and discomforts of war, kept me from bemoaning my lot inordinately.[6]

Emmanuelli's mother visited him often while he was in the camp, in spite of the long journey from the family home in Stoke-on-Trent. She was able to bring food parcels with her when she came, and was also on friendly terms with the landlady of the guesthouse at which she stayed, so much so that his mother could send her money to buy parcels for him. After many letters on his behalf, he finally received a tribunal hearing in London.

As more and more of the internees in Douglas were processed and released, it became possible to concentrate those who remained into fewer camps. The accommodation which thus became available was used not just for officer training but also by the Royal Navy.

In July 1941 a Royal Naval radar training school was established at the Douglas Head Hotel, with accommodation in the Regent and Granville hotels on Douglas Promenade, which were thenceforth known as HMS *Valkyrie*. Sid Toone was among those naval ratings posted to the station for training. In his memoirs he wrote:

> Our next place of training was HMS *Valkyrie* at Douglas on the Isle of Man where they had the full radar sets which were still secret. We were given rooms in hotels on the sea front, Loch Promenade, to our amazement next to hotels behind barbed wire! These were occupied by German, Italian and Japanese men internees! I couldn't believe it; we used to go to the highly secret Radar Training Quarters each day and these men (our enemies!) so near practised juggling and acrobatics behind their wire! Why didn't they have the radar base in Scotland, or move the enemy up there? I suppose that's how we won the war. The women internees were on the other side of the island at Port Erin, what a lovely hideout for spies this island was! The training got intense and of course it was a crash course to train

as many mechanics as possible for the newly-installed sets going on all our ships. But we had breaks in the evenings at the 'Onchan Hotel' doing the *Okey Cokey* (which was banned and the Hotel doors were shut), we visited the famous Glens, Ramsey, and other beauty spots on our Sundays off. ...Back on the radar course a week later, with another class, not so friendly, we were shown the latest battleship radar, No. 285. The instructor was (at the time) the only Chief Petty Officer Radar Mechanic in the Navy and he explained its working and range. He said the set could pick up aircraft at about 20 miles to 25 yards, and one of our chaps sarcastically said, 'I should have thought you could have seen a plane at 25 yards!' The C.P.O. didn't like this remark, and with a screwdriver in his hand stepped back into the open workings of the set. There was a blinding flash, 8,000 volts but only a few milliamps, and things went quiet. Fortunately all was well, and he carried on with his lecture. A few days later we were taken one at a time into a darkened room where a Lieutenant tried to panic each rating he tested by saying the answers to the type of repair questions that they would carry out were wrong. This was to see how you would react in extreme circumstances at sea.[7]

So secret was radar, and so paranoid were the authorities about keeping it from the enemy, that many Douglas residents had no idea what was going on under their noses. Indeed, so deeply was the ethos of secrecy ingrained into the recruits that only relatively recently have any spoken of it in any detail. This cloak of silence has only served to further conspiracy theories about what else was going on at Douglas Head. It is certainly true that radar was discovered accidentally in the 1930s by scientists who were actually searching for the government's idea of a 'death ray' capable of destroying ships and aircraft remotely. One theory has it that they were still trying to perfect the idea in the Isle of Man, using the radio equipment to project a concentrated beam onto Douglas Bay. After the war, the *Isle of Man Times* was allowed to visit the complex, perhaps to debunk some of these theories, and reported:

The buildings which comprise the Radar school include the Douglas Head Hotel, which was the first building to be fitted with Radar sets and classrooms, and which has been extended to accommodate further classrooms. Collinson's café, on the Head, has also been conditioned for Radar teaching and fitted with sets, and the Incline Railway ticket office has been fitted as a Radar operating room, and at one time even the platform used by the Douglas Head pierrots came into the Radar set-up. Six prefabricated huts have been built by the Navy and are used as classrooms, workshops, and a cinema, in which talkie pictures are shown to men on the first day of their course so that they can get a grounding in the general use of Radar equipment. A new three-storey block of buildings near the hotel contains 18 classrooms and numerous Radar sets... We saw classes being instructed in the use of Radar with high-angle and other guns, saw how the target is picked up on the dial and a bearing given, and the information passed on to Control. Then, when the target comes within range, the guns are trained on it, and with a movement of the foot a lever is pressed and the guns are fired, everything being timed so that the shell will be just where the enemy ship or aircraft is at the same time.

Another very interesting object was the plan position indicator, which is in the shape of a circle, and one looks down at it and sees, with the ship as the centre of the circle, any object coming within range of the Radar set. The P.P.I., as it is called, marks this object with a dot, and as the range and bearing are also indicated on it, one can see at a glance the direction of this object and its distance from the ship.

Other most interesting exhibits were models of the operations room on a battleship, very like an R.A.F. operations room in the set-up: the aircraft direction room, through which planes are first spotted, and the guns trained – actually the personnel here can have the guns trained on the target without orders. Then there is the Radar room, where the ratings listen to the heart-beats of the ship's Radar installations, and can tell at once when something goes wrong with one of them... This was our first visit since 1941 to that part of Douglas Head which was once the playground of thousands of visitors to the Island, and is now the training-ground of the Radar men. In the years between, no unauthorised person has been allowed to set foot inside this home of many secrets, which has been surrounded by barbed wire, and men of the Admiralty Civil Police, recruited locally, have been on guard day and night. But the giant masts and the small basket-like aerials have been prominent landmarks all that time.[8]

The most famous resident of HMS *Valkyrie* was undoubtedly the actor Jon Pertwee, later to become a household name as 'Dr Who' on television. As a 22-year-old naval lieutenant, however, he was at the start of his acting career and the Isle of Man provided him with

The actor Jon Pertwee in naval uniform during the Second World War. He was stationed at HMS Valkyrie *in Douglas. (BBC archives)*

many opportunities to develop his talent. He wrote afterwards that the beautiful Gaiety Theatre, just a stone's throw from his accommodation, was his inspiration to form a company of local amateurs and servicemen, among whom there were a number of professionals:

> My first production for 'The Service Players', as the company came to be known, was *Night Must Fall* by Emlyn Williams...as I had always wanted to play Danny. But as my Welsh accent was not of the best quality, I decided to play it in Cockney and it seemed to work. The following 'critique' was to me no ordinary one, written as it was by the ex-editor of the *Yorkshire Post*, Mr George Brown. As such it gave me tremendous heart and encouragement at that time, and also during the ensuing years. Of my performance as Danny, in *Night Must Fall*, Mr Brown said:
> 'Danny, played by a Sub-Lieutenant in the RNVR named Pertwee was really magnificent. Having seen the

play in London, and having seen it on the films, we would give Mr Pertwee's portrayal of Danny as the best of them. He has before him a fine future on the English stage.'

My co-producer was Sub-Lieutenant Jack Williams RNVR, now a most eminent television director. Among the cast was one professional opera singer, Norah Moore (no relation), and one professional actor, an old friend, Kenneth Henry, who played Inspector Belsize. Mrs Bramson was played by Olga Cowell, the wife of a respected lawyer in Douglas, Robert Cowell, who was also the Steward of the Isle of Man TT. This magnificent grande dame, for she could only be so described, could wipe the floor with 95 per cent of all the professional character actresses I have seen. She was in the Dame May Whitty/Margaret Rutherford mould, and with her grace and impeccable timing was a joy to work with. A tall, statuesque, bosomy lady, she carried herself with tremendous dignity and, like many large people, her feet positively twinkled. A turn around the dance floor with Olga was an experience not to be missed. She also played the piano with great flair and skill, a rare talent that I shamelessly tried to include into whatever play we were doing at the time. For many years I tried to persuade Olga Cowell to turn professional, but she would have none of it. 'Nonsense dear, I'm just a second-rate amateur, no one would ever employ me,' she said. In every play we presented she received notices from the critics that should have convinced her otherwise, but she was adamant and stayed an amateur.[9]

By 1941 a new buzz-phrase was on everyone's lips: 'IOM Go To It.' The expression was originally coined by Minister of Supply Herbert Morrison, and locally it was taken to sum up the new attitude that the island was ready and able to step up to the challenges of the conflict. In many ways, however, the Isle of Man was slow to awaken to the realities of war. The Manx people were among the last to get gas masks, the authorities claiming that the people of the island did not want them and only backing down following a campaign by the *Isle of Man Times*. Likewise its response to the need for air-raid precautions had been slow, and it was not until August 1941 that a dedicated Civil Defence Commission was set up. Ironically it was their great peacetime rival, Blackpool, which provided the Manx with the model of and impetus for proper ARP arrangements. The Lancashire resort was held up as an example of what could and should be done, and certainly a journalist from Blackpool noticed the contrast when visiting the island:

> The boat is different. Gone is the white paint, the holiday air. The first thing you get is a cork and canvas life belt. If you are in uniform you carry it by order. As a mere civilian your life is your own affair, and you probably leave the thing in the salon or littering the deck... Unless you have booked accommodation there will be difficulty, but the porters are still there, and the same taxi cabs await the unwary. They overcharge as ever... Some people in Douglas say the Island does not know there is a war on. In some respects this is true. Only now are serious efforts being made to institute a proper system of civil defence.[10]

Newspapers commented furiously on the refusal of the Manx people to heed the official warnings regarding ARP precautions, one commenting

> it is a fact (and a very disturbing one) that there is still, even at this stage of the war, a considerable number of incredibly stupid householders and business folk in Douglas who sit indoors listening to the late radio programmes, or reading the newspaper, sublimely indifferent to the tell-tale chinks of light which glow from their windows on to the street and into the sky.
>
> Again and again the Manx newspapers have drawn attention to this folly... Again and again the Police have hauled offenders into Court to be fined. Yet, apparently, there are many peculiar minds (if such they can be called) which can't grasp the significance of the warnings or the penalties.[11]

Yet in spite of frequent air-raid sirens, which indicated enemy aircraft in the vicinity and which required civil defence personnel to man their posts, there was no intentional hostile bombing of the Isle of Man. The first – and only – victim of the Luftwaffe on

'First victim of the Luftwaffe': a Manx frog that was burned to death in heather set alight by a stray German incendiary bomb. (Courtesy of Manx National Heritage)

the island, a frog that was charred to death in burning heather, was killed by an incendiary dropped by an off-course bomber. Nevertheless, its death had made front-page headlines on the island. Other bombs dropped harmlessly on Ballanard Road in Douglas and at Scarlett, while another damaged roof tiles at Laxey. In most cases it seems that the enemy aircraft was perhaps heading for Belfast and was lost.

Radar was a classic illustration of the adage that any sufficiently advanced technology can appear to be magic, and during the Second World War many people were usure where the line between the two was drawn. In October 1941 Dr Alexander Cannon, under threat of ejection by the army, finally left his home at Ballamoar, Jurby. Cannon was a quack doctor and charlatan who, with two dubious female assistants, had claimed to be able to use electricity to cure a variety of ailments. He had been visited the previous month by a journalist who wrote:

> His Excellency Alexander Cannon, K.G.S.L., Kushog Yogi of Northern Tibet, is to be thrown out of his castle in the Isle of Man. A platoon of soldiers will do it. For

the castle is wanted for important national purposes, and the requisitioning papers have now taken the form of an ejectment order. 'His Excellency' is regarded as the Mystery Man of the Island. To his palatial home Ballamoar – a castle only since he bought it – come wealthy men and women from England for treatment of all kinds of nervous diseases. The treatment varies a great deal, but includes hypnotism and occult methods. To-day I followed the road those patients take. It led me to an ornate gateway and then along a drive half a mile long up to the front door. I passed through a hall which was packed with Eastern images, with figures of the Buddha. Eastern gods and Chinese temples.

I waited in the lounge, which seemed like a miniature Eastern temple. A smell of incense permeated the room. On the walls were curious texts inscribed as 'translations': one of them said 'He is delightful to show kindness to youth and all His disciples are like a bunch of beautiful and fragrant peach flowers.' I was ushered into a room circular in shape, illuminated by a kind of searchlight which shone on the ceiling with a dull, red glow. 'His Excellency', Dr. Alexander Cannon, K.G.S.L., Kushog Yogi of Northern Tibet, rose to greet me. He doesn't look like a mystic. He is well-built, rather fleshy about the jowl, wears the biggest butterfly collar and the biggest black tie I have ever seen. I explained that I understood he was being ejected from this palatial country mansion. He agreed, protesting bitterly that he was the victim of personal animosity on the part of high authorities in the Isle of Man. As we talked aeroplanes passed closely overhead. I wondered why 'His Excellency' should have established a home for nervous cases at this particular point. He showed me a number of letters he had received sympathising with him because of the order to quit. One of them was signed by Sir Roger Keyes, who had written to the Governor of the Isle of Man asking if it were possible for other arrangements to be made. I asked him on what grounds he called himself 'Excellency'. He said it was a title conferred upon him by the Government of France.[12]

If even half of the stories surrounding Cannon are true, then he was a remarkable man. He had been Director of Public Health

Dr Alexander Cannon, the infamous 'yogi' who was believed to be a spy. He claimed to be able to read Hitler's brainwaves. (Author's collection)

in Hong Kong before returning to private practice in Harley Street. Conspiracy theorists allege that he was secretly treating the future King Edward VIII for a psychological problem, possibly alcoholism, and he is certainly mentioned by name in a letter from Archbishop of Canterbury Cosmo Gordon Lang on this subject. They further claim that for this reason, and for the embarrassment that he might cause the Royal family, he was forced by the establishment into exile on the Isle of Man.

Cannon's claims regarding his abilities grew wilder and wilder and shortly after the outbreak of war, he stated that he had equipment which allowed him to detect 'brainwaves'. He further claimed that he could tap into the thoughts of the Führer. In the tense wartime atmosphere the Manx police grew increasingly concerned by his activities. They wondered if the 'equipment' could be reversed, and if Cannon might actually be sending messages telepathically to Germany. Their suspicions were heightened when he had a line of trees on his property cut down, allowing him an uninterrupted view of RAF Jurby. MI5 was also tapping his phone and compromising telephone conversations were recorded, convincing the authorities that it was time to act. The saga was not yet over, however, because Cannon's new home was to be none other than Billown mansion, near Castletown, the grounds of which gave a good view over RAF Ronaldsway! In the post-war years Cannon continued to live quietly on the Isle of Man in his final residence, Laureston Manor in Douglas. To those privileged to have seen the interior, it bore all the hallmarks of a shrine to eastern mysticism, but Cannon spent his last years in modest fashion performing conjuring tricks and stage hypnotism.

More secrets were kept at the Douglas Bay Hotel, which at this time was used for the training of ATS girls who were attached to the Royal Corps of Signals. The nature of the activity here was so highly classified that even some forty years later, participants were reluctant to talk about it for fear of breaching the Official Secrets Act. One who did write about it stated:

> We didn't do codebreaking, but were part of 'Enigma/ Ultra', as we spent our time listening in to the Germans' wireless signals & took down their messages (in code) which were then sent on to Bletchley Park for the codebreakers to do their bit. I guess most of the wireless traffic was from the German Army – we were never told much! And, of course we were sworn to secrecy. We'd started learning the Morse code soon after being chosen for this program & had intensive sessions in becoming 'fluent' in taking Morse before actually 'going on ops' in England.[13]

Just along the headland from the Douglas Bay Hotel was the Howstrake Holiday Camp. In the early part of the war it (along with Cunningham's Holiday Camp) had been used to house the boy sailors of the naval training school HMS *St George*, but by mid-1941 was home to the Junior Wing of the Royal Naval School of Music, the boys who were in training to become Royal Marine bandsmen. One of them, Don Flounders, remembered:

> Shore Leave, as it was known from the moment we joined, was available from 1 p.m. on Saturdays and Sundays and expired at 10 p.m. The 'Manx Electric Railway' ran right past the camp and was the easiest way to get into Douglas, the largest town... Following the tram's arrival at its terminus, the eager mass of Band Boys emerged from the terminal and streamed along the seafront towards the fleshpots of the town. Whilst not exactly flush with money (I think at that time I was getting 8 shillings a week, but I could be wrong), prices were low and tightly controlled so what we did have went quite a long way. My usual Saturday run ashore was typical of most of the boys and went much as follows. First call would be at a cake shop where I always purchased two custard tarts, receiving them in a

brown paper bag. It was then straight to one of the town's cinemas to catch the matinee. It didn't much matter what was showing but the programme would typically consist of a news bulletin, a cartoon or two, a not very long minor film (known as a 'B' film) and then the main feature. We would sit there, warm and comfortable, munching on our custard tarts, cakes, buns, etc., carefully keeping the paper bag for a long-established special purpose. Love scenes of those days were very reserved and sanitised, but no matter what the subject matter, there was always at least one 'steamy' moment. Unsuspecting patrons would be sitting absorbed in the film, as the hero and heroine's lips moved towards the kiss. Had anyone been listening for it, at that moment there would be surreptitious rustling and sounds of exhaled breath, followed, at the exact moment lips met, with bangs and pops from all over the cinema as we burst our inflated paper bags. Angry protests would sometimes erupt from a few startled patrons, but the management never tried to stop it, as long as the habit remained confined to matinees only. After all, Band Boys will be Band Boys!

The film over, it was time to head for the 'Sally Gash', more properly known as the Salvation Army Canteen, where good-hearted and worthy ladies provided at a minimal price the ammunition necessary to fill young stomachs. Sausage, chips, baked beans, fried eggs with tea and a slice of bread. Wonderful stuff. Replete for once, we would then retrace our steps and head for one of the other cinemas, just in time for the evening session. That finished (and no paper bags), we would emerge, this time into the blackout and (some of us, dare I admit it?) head for a pub known for its laxity in enforcing the minimum age laws. The phrase 'if you're old enough to be in uniform, you're old enough to drink' was commonplace during the war. A quick pint or half-pint later (depending on the state of finances) and it was to the fish and chip shop to purchase a goodly newspaper-wrapped packet of hot chips. Especially appreciated in winter with the wind howling in off the sea, the packet, tucked inside our greatcoats, would keep us warm as we munched chips all the way along the 'prom' back to the tram terminal. Once there it was time for some fun and games with the local 'bad' girls. There would usually be at least four or five and were known as P.T.s (you work it out). They would lead a lad on and then run off just when things got interesting. Some of them had picturesque and self-descriptive nicknames. 'The Onchan Basher' and 'Laxey Lou' still spring to mind.[14]

The year ended with news that blackout restrictions would be lifted slightly to allow the hunting of rabbits at night with lamps, provided this was done carefully and in some cases under military supervision. This was in the main because rabbits had become such a problem that they were destroying whole crops, particularly in the north of the island. Indeed so bad had the situation become that farmers were advised to approach known poachers to assist them with the work! The change in regulations also allowed those hunting rabbits to enter on to any private land, with or without the owner's consent. The fur of the creatures was widely sought after for clothing purposes, and they also provided a valuable source of protein as 'off the ration' meat.

The festive season made separation from loved ones all the more poignant. Because they were confined to bed by illness, Mr and Mrs Lewis Killip of Laxey did not hear the radio message broadcast to them by their only son, Trooper Alan Killip of the Royal Armoured Corps, in the 'Greetings from Cairo' feature on Christmas Eve. The message was, however, heard by Mr Clayton, a friend and neighbour, who went at once to the Killips' house, only to find that they had not known that a Laxey man had been announced as taking part in the programme and had not switched on their radio set. He nonetheless relayed Alan's message, and assured them that his familiar voice sounded robust. Naturally they were deeply disappointed at having missed their son's words. Moreover the messages on Christmas Eve were broadcast from the surgical ward in a military hospital, where wounded from the Western Desert campaign were being treated, and this was the first indication that he was injured. However, his message concluded reassuringly: 'Hope you are well and happy. I am fine.' Killip, who had joined the army as a regular before the war, had been recalled to the colours in 1939. He received his wound at Tobruk, where he also was awarded the Military Medal. His parents would not have long to wait until they saw him again, however, for the

Trooper Alan Killip MM of the Royal Armoured Corps, awarded the Military Medal in North Africa. (Courtesy of Barry Bridson)

following year he was a patient at Nobles, undergoing further treatment for his arm injury before discharge.

Christmastime, particularly in this early part of the war, also presented an unprecedented challenge to the Castletown Brewery. Syd Cringle who worked there remembered:

The influx of service personnel to the island put an impossible strain on the brewery to meet the demands that occurred at Christmas... Firstly we were restricted in the quantity we could brew, due to the shortage of materials and the limited fermenting space then available. Fermentation, ideally, takes seven days, so that a fermenting vat is tied up for this period. To expedite supplies we worked on a six days' fermentation which, while not ideal, enabled us to speed up brewing a little. Secondly, there was a shortage of bottles and cases. I can remember...working until one a.m. on Christmas Day bottling beer and fitting the bottles into large chests on the back of RAF lorries, as this was the only way to satisfy the messes at RAF Jurby.[15]

Those in the messes perhaps had some justification for their thirst, because by the end of 1941 the initial period of panic had passed. Although blackout restrictions and ARP measures were strictly enforced, invasion had not come and Britain (including the Isle of Man) had settled into the job of fighting the war. There were even chinks of light ahead in that the USSR had not collapsed in the face of the ferocious German attack in the summer (in the process turning Stalin into an unlikely British hero, his jovial 'Uncle Joe' persona being completely at odds with reality), while the Japanese attack on Pearl Harbor in December had brought the United States into the war on Britain's side. In the coming year Britain and her allies would begin, little by little, to turn the tide.

CHAPTER FOUR

1942: Ringing of Church Bells

The year of 1942 was arguably the turning-point of the war. It would prove in the end to have been its mid-point and, like a fulcrum, the course of the global conflict balanced upon it. Up to this stage, the war had in the main gone the way of the Axis powers, but in 1942 things began – albeit slowly – to tip against them. At the desert railway halt of El Alamein, the British and Commonwealth forces in North Africa finally defeated the German and Italian forces under Rommel. Churchill would go on to say, not entirely accurately, that before El Alamein Britain never had a victory and that afterwards she never had a defeat. Meanwhile in the east, German forces reached Stalingrad in what would prove to be the high watermark in their campaign against the Soviet Union. Following the Japanese attack on Pearl Harbor, the empire of the rising sun made some early gains in the Far East. However, the United States also now came into the war on the side of Britain, and though it would take some time before the full weight of its military and industrial muscle could be brought to bear, this would prove a decisive factor.

Some US help had already started to trickle through, however. In January of 1942 an American named James S. Farrior was posted to RAF Scarlett, the radar site near Castletown. Farrior was from Alabama and although he wore RAF-style uniform, he was in fact a member of the Civilian Technical Corps (CTC). The members of this formation were recruited throughout the USA from university students with a knowledge of physics, radio station technicians and others of a similar bent in order to provide the specialist staff to man the expanding Chain Home system. Farrior kept a fascinating diary of his experiences on the Isle of

Man, and it records the sense of wonder with which this young man from the Deep South encountered the winding streets of Castletown and the ancient headstones in churchyards. He also records that the main form of entertainment for airmen and soldiers based around Castletown was a visit to the Cosy Cinema, where the cigarette smoke in the small auditorium was so thick during a performance that it burned his eyes.

RAF Scarlett had four 325ft steel guyed towers that supported the two sets of transmitting curtain arrays (Main and Standby). There were also two 240ft self-supporting towers made of wood. These supported the receiving dipoles and had to be climbed at regular intervals for inspection; not a job for the faint-hearted. In February

James S. Farrior, a member of the Civilian Technical Corps (CTC). He worked at RAF Scarlett Chain Home radar station. (Courtesy of Manx National Heritage)

of that year, maintenance was required on one of the curtain arrays and although it did not require climbing, it was still a tedious job. Farrior writes:

> This morning, despite the cold, damp, windy weather, we had to take down the curtain array from the 325 foot towers near T Block-1 to make a repair and to clean the insulators. Letting it down with the winch was a slow process, and after it was down, we had to spread it out on the ground so we could work on it. The towers are located near the edge of the sea, and the cold wind was blowing directly off the sea. It was a miserable day of work.
>
> We got the array down, made the repair, and cleaned the insulators. Putting it back up was not easy, as everything had to be kept untangled as the array was cranked back up. When it was finally back in place, we examined it with

a telescope and found to our dismay that some of the open wire feeders had become twisted. That meant that it must come down again. The work had not been finished when I got off at 5pm.

We have a standby transmitter block, T Block-2, which has an identical MB2 transmitter and curtain array that we use when the main one is being repaired. In a field to the east of the transmitting towers used with T Block-2, is a dummy (decoy) transmitter block. It is not actually a block, but is something made to look like a poorly camouflaged block. Sometimes, when an inexperienced radio mechanic arrives at Scarlett, the location of the dummy block is pointed out, and he is directed to 'go there and assist the mechanic who is repairing the dummy MB2 transmitter.' If he is a 'dummy' radio mechanic, he will go there before he realizes that it is a joke.[1]

RAF Scarlett would eventually be closed due to the expansion of the airfield at Ronaldsway, because its 325ft aerial masts were well inside the mandatory 6,000 yard construction limit. The station was mothballed shortly after the completion of a new facility, RAF Dalby at Niarbyl, later in 1942, though both ran simultaneously for a time to ensure unbroken cover. With the closure of Scarlett, and Bride around the same time, Dalby remained the only CH station on the island for the remainder of the war. Although radar was still highly secret, it was rumoured among the technical staff that it had thus far had a great impact on the course of the war, and was responsible for the decrease in German bombing raids launched against Britain. Certainly the Isle of Man's CH stations played a key role in protecting the north-west from aerial incursions. The Irish Sea, it was believed, represented a particular risk in terms of air attack because it was thought that German bombers could use the signal of Radio Éireann (later RTE) out of Dublin for navigation purposes. It was strongly rumoured that Dalby also incorporated a dummy transmitting station, which bounced the Radio Éireann signal back again in order to confuse the bombers.

However, at this time the threat from Japan in the Far East, where there was no early-warning system, grew ever greater. Having attacked Pearl Harbor in December the previous year and overrun Hong Kong at Christmas, in February 1942 she

A view of the aerial masts at RAF Dalby (Niarbyl), a Chain Home radar station which replaced that at Scarlett. The steel masts in the foreground stood some 300ft tall. The somewhat shorter wooden masts closer to the shore were decoys. (Courtesy of John Hall)

finally launched her long anticipated attacks against Malaya and Burma. Captain Bruce Toothill was serving in the latter region as a captain in the 7th Battalion, 10th Baluch Regiment. He was the son of a Douglas businessman and after being educated at King William's College had gone to work in India. Like many British ex-pats with a knowledge of Hindi or other local languages, he was given an emergency commission in the Indian army. His

Captain Bruce Toothill, 7/10th Baluch Regiment, Indian army. After capture in Malaya, he spent the remainder of the war as a prisoner of the Japanese in Rangoon jail. (Courtesy of Manx National Heritage)

battalion was quickly overrun in the initial Japanese attack, and in notes prepared in captivity which he wrote up after the war, he gave an account of the one-sided battle in which he was captured:

The Subedar Major, a fine old soldier, tried to throw a grenade, but they were too close to him and he was bayonetted before he had a chance. The rest surrendered so I found myself in the centre of a circle of roughly 25 yards radius looking down the wrong end of a dozen rifles. It was a queer feeling – I loaded my pistol with a hand which I won't claim was steady and yet I recall my main thought was curiosity – how was it going to end and what would it be like on the Other Side?

I was not kept long in doubt. The fight lasted only a few minutes. Had they been Germans and better shots it should not have lasted more than seconds. The first bullet got me through the leg, just above the ankle; the second, a couple of minutes later, scraped my shoulder; the third knocked the smile off my face in no uncertain fashion, removing fourteen teeth and breaking my jaw prior to leaving via my left cheek – I am afraid I packed in at that stage as I felt as if I had tried to kiss an express train. I did not lose consciousness and asked a Japanese soldier by signs to finish me off as life did not appeal very much and I did not want to be left to the vultures. This he refused to do. Time alone will show whether he was doing me a good turn.

It is most unusual for the Japanese to bother to take wounded prisoners and I have never been able to find out why they showed me this consideration. I was useless for purposes of interrogation as the bullet nicked my tongue and for a week I could only gobble like a goose...probably it was because I had a few of my own troops with me who could act as stretcher-bearers – the stretcher consisting of two pieces of bamboo, across which some of our signal wire was stretched.[2]

He was taken eventually to Rangoon jail where, despite the neglect of his wounds by the Japanese, he recovered. Only the gaping gash in his left cheek caused him problems when eating, and he had to hold this together with his hand. It would be a testament to the skill developed by British plastic surgeons during the war that they would eventually be able to rebuild his face.

Bandsman Gordon Cowley, Royal Marines. He was born and grew up in Douglas, and after training at Howstrake Camp was posted to HMS *Edinburgh. (Courtesy of Gordon Cowley)*

Manxman Gordon Cowley would soon also join the war against Japan in the Far East but his first posting, after undergoing training as a Royal Marine bandsman at Howstrake camp, was to HMS *Edinburgh*. At sea, Royal Marine bandsmen operated the transmitting room, deep inside the ship, directing the fire of the turrets. After further training, the ship went out into the Atlantic to meet convoys coming back from the USA, before joining an Arctic convoy bound for Murmansk. Once in the northern Russian port, something unusual occurred:

> Just before we were due to leave...a train with trucks came alongside and out jumped a whole load of Russian soldiers... unloading wooden crates... There are no staircases on a warship, only ladders, and they were lowering these down when one slipped away and burst open, and out came these gold bars.[3]

The cargo, valued at around £50 million today, was Stalin's part-payment for arms and supplies sent to Russia in the early period of the war. The wooden crates were stencilled in red lettering and in the rain this had begun to run, giving the appearance of blood. For the British sailors it seemed like a bad omen. Cowley takes up the story again:

> Sure enough we had only got out about 200 miles on the return journey when a submarine got us with two torpedoes on the starboard side. Where the band was, was right down in the very bottom of the ship. When this happened, I'd just come off the afternoon watch at at 4 o'clock, and I'd just gone up 10 minutes or quarter of an hour and BANG. So fortunately I wasn't down below at this time. This submarine got us with two in the starboard side, and we went over about 17 degrees straight away. It kind of lifted it. Although it was about 11,000 tons you still felt it reverberate. The funny thing was (not then!) that I couldn't swim and we used to have these blow-up lifebelts, and I was so excited that I unscrewed [the valve] too far and the washer fell out somewhere. I screwed it back up and tried to blow it up! I said to the corporal, 'I can't blow it up!' He said, 'You're alright, I haven't got one myself!' So this old shoe I had had a rubber sole that was a bit worn, so I managed to cut a bit and make a washer, fortunately, but it was about minus 10 and after five minutes [in the water] you would have been gone. But two small minesweepers came alongside; there were 800 of us, and 400 roughly got on each. I laugh about it now, but I didn't at the time. To get to it I had to get up a ladder, two or three decks and came out through a hatchway. The damage-control people were hammering shut the watertight doors, closing the cleats, and several men were killed as a result of being shut in, as we got to the top they were starting to shut it, but we banged and banged on it and they let us through. And as I got through that, I was going past the wardroom and somebody shouted, 'Come here, help this wounded man.' So two of us got this man who could hardly walk, an arm each, and as we did so they shouted, 'Make way for the wounded!' so about 800 people parted, and from being about number 800 to get off we must have been in the first hundred! I held on to him until our feet were on this other ship, the *Gossamer*.[4]

Saving the Russian gold was the last thing on the minds of the crew, and when a British destroyer finally sank the crippled *Edinburgh* the gold went down with her. The crew were returned to Murmansk where they spent about eight weeks in a Russian barracks on a diet of pine tea, raw fish and other unpalatable offerings before coming back to the UK.

The North Russian convoys were not the only challenges facing the British Royal and Merchant navies. They were also heavily committed to keeping Malta resupplied, and that spring a series of attempts had been made to reach the island in the face of pitiless air attacks by the Luftwaffe and Regia Aeronautica (Italian Royal Air Force). After heavy losses earlier in the summer, Operation PEDESTAL became a critical make-or-break bid to get fuel supplies through. Another young Manx sailor, Able Seaman Robert Kinnin, reported in a letter home to his parents (Mr and Mrs Kinnin of 6 Cooper's Lane, Ramsey) that for three days and nights this convoy was attacked in the Mediterranean by a terrific concentration of bombers, E-boats and submarines. Seaman Kinnin wrote of the 'bombing hell' that the enemy kept up against his destroyer and described how the tanker *Ohio* was torpedoed. Three destroyers including his own ship attempted to assist the tanker and another ship which had been hit, but had to let go owing to the fierce onslaught by a group of Stuka dive-bombers. Later, instructions came to save the tanker if possible and two destroyers manoeuvred alongside:

> We were strapped to her for two days and three nights. We were half-carrying, half-towing her at six knots... I prayed that a U-boat wouldn't hit us with a 'tin fish', as the first time they hit her it was only in a tank which was full of heavy fuel, but the rest were filled with highly inflammable aviation spirit, and if they had hit her in one of these we would have all been cooked geese! Anyway, after all the action we had come through it seemed like a miracle – it really was a miracle, I think. They didn't attack us and we arrived in Malta... We staggered into Malta harbour, and there was a brass band up on Valletta playing – of all things – *A Life on the Ocean Wave*! Lord Gort was there chucking his hat in the air.[5]

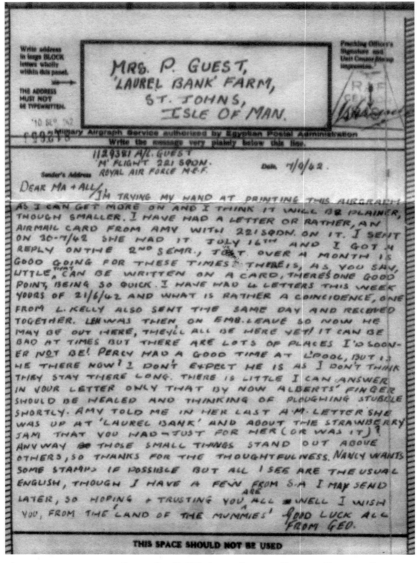

An aerogramme sent home by RAF Aircraftsman George Guest to his mother at Laurel Bank farm. (Author's collection)

Back at home, the shortages of imported food supplies meant that every effort was being made to get the most out of the land under cultivation. A Manx Women's Land Army had been started about a year previously, and one of the earliest recruits was Laura Briggs who had spent much of her early life on a farm. After some further training in agriculture at the government's experimental station at Knockaloe, she was sent to work for Mr Eddie Kneen at Ballamona, Ballaugh. There her main tasks involved milking and cleaning out cows, and initially there was no uniform provided. She recalled that at first she used her father's overalls, which her mother cut down and as he was a tall man, there was quite a lot of excess. Even though Laura would tie them round the middle as best she could, the main impression she gave as she went out into the field with the horse and cart was of a peculiar sort of scarecrow. So it was rather a red-letter day when, in 1942, uniform was finally provided:

> Everything we got was beautiful, the boots were brown leather, they were beautiful boots, wellies, of course, and then woolly socks, riding breeches... And hats, we had aertex shirts, beige aertex shirts, that was for working in, and beautiful v-necked green pullovers, those really were very high standard... There was what we would call a car coat now, which was our coat over... In the summer time we had khaki dungarees.[6]

Knockaloe was also the scene of a tragic wartime accident one day in June 1942. Ann Moore was living on the Isle of Man with her mother in order to be near her father Leading Aircraftsman Albert Snelsdon, who was a member of staff at No. 5 Aerial Observers' School at RAF Jurby. One morning, after her father had waved cheerily to them as he left the house that they were renting in Sulby, events took a shocking turn for the little girl. Taken to a stranger's house, she was ushered into the garden while the adults talked indoors:

> Sitting in the quiet garden, I suddenly felt cold. Something was wrong. The stranger was too kind, and why had mother not spoken? It was if she hadn't even known I was there. Mickey Mouse waved at me from the front of

the comic, but I didn't want to read and it slipped from my knee. I didn't want to drink either. I sat frozen in the sunshine, twisting [my] necklace at my throat and trying not to feel sick... The minutes ticked by and the butterflies in my stomach seemed to become dragonflies, whirring, pressing painfully against me, inside. I twisted the necklace tighter and it snapped, collapsing into my hand. Tears pricked my eyes. What was happening? What was wrong? It was as if the sun had suddenly lost its warmth or gone behind the clouds, and everything was so quiet. Only a faint breeze whispered in the leaves beside me. Then the woman appeared again.

'Come along, dear,' she said, holding out her hand. 'I'm going to take you and mother home.' I looked at the broken necklace, wordlessly... Nothing was said on the journey home, but I was to find that my stricken mother had suddenly become a widow.[7]

Her father had been part of the crew of a Blenheim bomber undertaking a training exercise with another aircraft, flying over Knockaloe Farm south of Peel. For reasons which were never discovered, the two had made contact, causing them to crash in nearby farmland with the loss of both crews. The propeller of one of the aircraft went through the wall of Patrick schoolroom, but fortunately there were no casualties among children or staff as it happened before school had begun. The scar from this incident can still be seen in the rebuilt school wall. Yet the sheer scale of air activity over the island made such accidents inevitable. Frank Cowin tells us of an incident at Douglas:

I remember actually seeing one [crash]... I was going along one day and there was a plane, it flew more or less between the lighthouse and the rocks and...it caught the rocks. I saw it go into a vertical climb and then stall. As it flipped downwards you could see something come out of it and fall. The plane crashed just on the bottom end of the battery near the inclined railway. The object I saw go out was the pilot, but his parachute didn't open and he was found on the rocks down at Port Skillion... There were so many planes buzzing around the place. There were Polish pilots training up at Andreas, and one of their favourite tricks was to come into Douglas and fly along the Promenade between the lamp posts, trying to scare the living daylights out of everybody. I suppose particularly aimed at the internees or prisoners of war, but it was quite fun. And then there were others, things like Beauforts which were training planes for navigators... If we were over near the Palace, there was a much bigger drop on to the beach there then, and they would be flying almost level with us as they went along over the beach. If they saw you wave to them, you would get a wave back from them, from the trainee navigators in the back. They brought Lysanders in and landed on the sand at the bottom of the beach when the tide was well out. That happened occasionally and a few times a flying boat came in and landed on the sea, I think a Walrus maybe and on another occasion a Catalina...and then at the weekends when we went to Sunday school we would often go for a walk along the harbour and very often you would see one or two of the very long low-loaders, with the remains of aircraft on them waiting to be shipped back across for salvaging whatever they could out of them.[8]

The nature of combat and wartime flying training meant that there were inevitably other accidents, particularly over the higher terrain of the Isle of Man. Sadly these are too numerous to describe in detail here. Training accidents also occurred in ground operations, as Syd Cringle remembered. Aged 17, he had joined the Home Guard, which by this stage in the war had reached quite a high level of efficiency. The most realistic exercise in which Cringle's platoon took part was a joint one with 208 OCTU, which was stationed in the Golf Links Hotel, Port St Mary. This was a night operation that took place on Stoney Mountain and the Eary Dam. After a good start to the exercise there was a serious accident, resulting in the deaths of a number of cadets. It later transpired that while one assault craft was crossing the dam, another was dropping charges into the water to simulate gunfire. By some mischance, all the charges in the second craft ignited at once, blowing it to pieces and killing those on board.

Cringle's platoon was based in Castletown, and he recalled that by now the Home Guard had discarded the shotguns and pikes with

The tailfin of a mortar bomb found in a field near Cregneash and almost certainly fired by members of 208 OCTU who trained in the area. (Courtesy of Manx National Heritage)

which it had first been armed and had been re-equipped with more modern weapons:

The HQ was in Castle Rushen. A guard was mounted nightly in a room just below the top of the highest tower. To me it seemed more like a fire-watch than a military guard post... The members were issued with American .300 calibre rifles (the basic army issue was .303 calibre). The bayonets on the .300 were the original long blades whereas the modern British rifle had only a six-inch spike... There was also a grenade-launcher and a weapon known as the 'Northover Projector'.

I had the dubious responsibility for using the grenade-launcher. In retrospect, I suppose being the youngest member I was adjudged to have the least sense! The launcher consisted of a .300 calibre rifle, reinforced around the barrel and the stock with a binding of copper wire. A metal cup that could accommodate a Mills Bomb with the lever in place was screwed onto the end of the barrel... I am pleased to say I never had to fire it as, to me, it always appeared to be a very dangerous weapon for our own side.[9]

The pressures of war would inevitably bring about some cracks in society. While many gave up what little free time they had to the Home Guard or AFS, those who were perceived not to be pulling their weight attracted the ire of correspondents of the local press such as W.H. Alcock MHK, who wrote:

Members of Castletown Home Guard. The platoon provided the guard for Castle Rushen. (Courtesy of Barry Bridson)

> This is no time to have a feather-bed outlook; it is now entirely a question of who has the absolutely last man for the fighting forces. The Tribunal can only deal with those who are brought before them. They cannot go out into the 'highways and the hedges' and search for shirkers. That is obviously the work for your anonymous correspondents who I am sure, are smarting at the sight of shirkers hiding under the words, 'Reserved Occupation'.[10]

Yet in spite of this kind of intense scrutiny that they might come under from their fellow citizens, conscientious objectors often received a more enlightened official response, sometimes surprisingly so. Cecil Cannell McFee, a plumber of Main Road, Colby, was one such. He was an ex-president of the Manx Labour

Party and a Methodist local preacher in the Castletown circuit. At a tribunal he stated:

> As a citizen of the Isle of Man, I try to serve the community in the sphere of the local preacher, and since the formation of the A.F.S. in our district I have served as a member, voluntarily, and in no way seek to avoid responsibility [but]...the war machine...is set in motion, and it seeks to destroy and break down, and another section of that machine is brought in to patch up and heal and stimulate the process of destruction. I could not take part in a machine of that kind... I look on the A.F.S. in the same way as I look upon the lifeboat or the fire service. Through it I can do something for the people with whom I live to save their lives, but not in any way that could affect my conscience.[11]

According to the report of this hearing some of the most sympathetic comments came from Major Keith Grimble Groves, the military representative. Lest this be thought an isolated incident, a short while later newspapers reported upon the case of another conscientious objector, Edward George Nicholls of Clugat Cottage, Sulby, employed by an English firm building the new reservoir at Block Eary, Sulby Glen. He had stated that he would resist medical examination at all costs, because military service was not in accord with the will of God, and had returned his call-up papers with a letter in which he wrote: '...as a Christian, I know the will of God, so it is impossible for me to attend for examination for military service. I know I am liable to a heavy penalty, but to remain in the will of God is all that really matters.'[12]

At a court hearing, Nicholls claimed that he was registered in England as a conscientious objector. Under cross-examination, he said he knew the scheme on which he was working provided water for people taking part in the war, but that was different to attending to an injured soldier, because in doing that he would be 'assisting in murder' and helping the military machine. Nicholls was subsequently taken in the custody of the police to the Military Division Offices in Douglas, where a special medical board had been convened for him. On arrival he informed the medical officers of his determination not to proceed with the examination, and he was then allowed to leave the building a free man. Although he was summoned to court one further time, the crown offered no evidence and the case against him was dropped.

In spite of perceptions of the Isle of Man as a sleepy backwater, events around the world frequently had repercussions for the island as ripples from these incidents washed up on its shores. The Allied invasion of faraway Madagascar, which like many French colonies had been pro-Vichy, resulted in September of 1942 in a request from the Foreign Office to billet captured French officers and their families on the Isle of Man. They were housed in Laxey and Baldrine, and were not permitted outside a specified radius from Laxey police station without the permission of Government Office. They were also subject to a curfew at night. Coming from the hot climate of Madagascar, these people felt the damp and cold of a Manx winter severely and had to have a special issue of blankets along with an extra ration of fuel. They remained

Edward Stowell, an income tax official who lived on St Ninian's Road, declared himself a conscientious objector when called up for Home Guard service. He had served in the First World War, but had been a member of the Methodist Peace Fellowship since 1938. (Courtesy of Alistair Ramsay)

under the authority of the senior officer, General Claerebout, but were allowed to use the shops in Laxey. The *Peel City Guardian* at the time reported that the group was not anti-British, but was in fact pro-Allied. It added that educational arrangements were being made for the numerous children, who had already begun to make friends among the locals. Their stay on the Isle of Man was to be short-lived, however, and the group left early the following year when their husbands agreed to serve with the Allied forces.

The enlightened attitude of the Manx authorities towards their wartime guests is nowhere better illustrated than in the case of Dr Gerhard Bersu. An eminent German archaeologist before the war, Bersu had fallen foul of the Nazi regime and in 1935 had been forced to step down from his position at the German Archaeological Institute. He and his wife came to Britain, and his excavation at Woodbridge in Suffolk had brought him to the attention of the British archaeological community. The outbreak of war had resulted in the pair being interned on the Isle of Man, separately at first but later in the married camp. The staff and trustees of the Manx Museum were aware of who Bersu was, and through their influence he was allowed to undertake excavations outside the camp, using internees as labour. These people for their part were only too willing to have something interesting to occupy their time. The unusual wartime conditions of plentiful free labour combined with an absence of time pressure resulted in high-quality archaeological work at three sites, and Bersu produced the first preliminary report in October 1942.

It focused upon his excavation at Ballakeigan where three Iron Age round houses had existed in consecutive periods. The report stated that initially there was a large timber building, roughly circular, 90ft in diameter, with an outer wall of very narrowly-set posts. From a wide entrance in the north-east a paved entrance hall, with a row of middle posts, led to a fireplace in the midst of the circle. The hearth was built up by big flags of Poolvaish limestone and surrounded by a thick clay floor. Six concentric rows of posts, with an opening at the entrance hall, divided the space between hearth and outer wall. The substance of the wood was sometimes well-preserved as rectangular stumps of bog oak. The report concluded:

> The period about 500 A.D. belongs to a very unknown part of the history of the British Isles. For the first time it is now known what the house of one of the little chieftains of this period looks like, and a picture about the conditions on the Isle of Man before the devastating raids of the Norse invasions is obtained. For the historian it is very important to see that near the coast, on a place near accessible harbours, wealthy people like the squires

Dr Gerhard Bersu, the German archaeologist who undertook pioneering excavation work on the Isle of Man while interned in Rushen camp.

of later times could live in a big unfortified house, in the open country, undisturbed by troublesome events through several generations.[13]

Archaeological techniques were less advanced in some areas than those of today and the bog oak, once its presence was noted, was considered to be of little further value. Thus it was that large amounts were used by the internees to make craft items for sale or as gifts, these ranging from cufflinks to brooches and even cigarette-holders.

Another incident with wide-ranging repercussions was the battle of El Alamein on the Egypt-Libya border. In November 1942 the island's church bells were rung for the first time in more than two years, not to signal an enemy invasion, but in thanksgiving for this victory. So unfamiliar was the sound that it set the dogs barking in Douglas. At St Matthew's, three little girls begged for the privilege of ringing the bells, which the good-

A Bofors anti-aircraft gun and its crew from the Manx Regiment in the Western Desert, 1942. (Courtesy of the Manx Aviation Preservation Society/Manx Regiment Museum)

natured verger allowed. The Manx Regiment was attached to an armoured division at El Alamein, and detailed for duty up the line near the edge of the Qattara Depression. Their first casualties occurred when one of their anti-aircraft guns received a direct hit from a shell. Two men were killed and five wounded. Later two men from Castletown were killed, and Major Brian Mylchreest and a sergeant were wounded. Major Mylchreest saw some Stukas coming over and lay on the ground watching them through his glasses. He actually saw the bombs leave the planes and called out to his gunners, 'These are ours.' The next thing he felt was the vibration of a bomb bursting and the place was shrouded in dust.

One bomb seemed to hit the gun by which he was lying, or burst close by it, causing a number of casualties, and the gun itself was badly damaged. Mylchreest later paid tribute to the efficiency of the medical service, saying that he was given morphia within ten minutes of being knocked out, and was in an ambulance being taken to the clearing station ten minutes later.

A number of other Manx soldiers were present, notably Hector Duff, who was in command of a scout car reconnoitring ahead of

German prisoners of war are searched for items that might provide intelligence information during the battle of El Alamein. (Library of Congress)

The watch taken from a dead German soldier at El Alamein by Manx soldier Hector Duff. (Courtesy of Manx National Heritage)

his regiment. Usually in these situations, they would try to capture a prisoner who might give them details of the enemy unit opposite. When none was available, they would search any enemy dead nearby. Hector remembered that the Afrika Korps soldiers would usually have photographs of their wives and children in their paybooks, just like their British counterparts. On this occasion, near Hemeimat, he also found a watch in a dead soldier's pocket and made a note to return it to the man's wife, as well as letting her know where he had died and that he had not suffered.

On the agricultural front, 1942 had seen an increase in the number of acres of land under crops, though the total population working on the land had decreased. A report produced in December included other interesting statistics concerning the agricultural effort. Although the number of horses was down slightly, there were still nearly 3,000 in use in agriculture at this time. While the total number of workers was down, there had been an increase in female labour with more than 200 women now working on Manx farms. Double Summer Time had been introduced in 1941, with the clocks (which had not been set back in the autumn of 1940) advanced a further hour. This move, however, was widely disapproved of by those in agriculture on the Isle of Man. Smallholder Adrian Wall wrote:

> There is much opposition to double summer-time from farmers on the island; their objections are not without foundation, as having regard to the heavy morning dews

experienced here the grass and corn get wet and hours
are lost in the morning at hay and harvest time caused
by the men having to stand by until the sun has done its
work, and on dull days frequently a morning's work is
lost; in consequence overtime has to be worked sometimes
at inconvenience to the farm hands. The cattle will not
recognise the altered time, G.M.T. being the foundation
of their lives; no one may interfere with their timetable.
The whole farm is thrown out of gear by it and agriculture
suffers in consequence. Last year during harvest time we
had many weeks' bad weather and yet the time for getting
in the harvest was shortened each day.[14]

The year ended with news of the loss of another Steam Packet
ship, HMS *Tynwald*, which had been absorbed into the Royal Navy
and converted into an anti-aircraft vessel. The *Isle of Man Times*,
in reporting the incident, stated that the Steam Packet Company
had now lost 9,385 tons of shipping thus far as a result of the
war. Although this was a serious matter, the underlying tone of
its report was upbeat and confident: 'These ships could not be
replaced to-day at double the cost, but their loss will be felt by
the whole island, because it is impossible to say when passenger-
carrying ships can be built after victory is won.'[15]

That month an important debate took place in Tynwald
regarding the role and performance thus far of the Manx War
Cabinet. Although the lieutenant governor was at pains to suggest
that the role of the War Committee (as it was also known) was
purely to advise him, others such as Deemster Percy Cowley
astutely observed that it was an important development in Manx
democracy and predicted that it would be retained in some form
in the post-war world. The coming year would see the British,
Americans and other Allied forces poised to finally roll up the
German and Italian positions in North Africa. The war in the
West would soon move to Europe once more.

This appeal on behalf of the Red Cross PoW fund gives a figure of 185 Manx men in enemy hands as of December 1942.

CHAPTER FIVE

1943: Tipping the Balance

The fourth year of the war, 1943 underlined the changing balance of power as Axis forces began to retreat on all fronts. The year was to witness the Allied invasion – and collapse – of Italy. As she sued for an armistice, this change in her status would have an effect upon the position of Italian internees on the Isle of Man (many of whom had by this stage in the conflict become something of a fixture). It would not, however, bring an end to fighting in Italy herself, where stubborn German resistance in the north continued. On the Isle of Man, there were also to be subtle changes in the balance of power: the year would see Tynwald challenge the Westminster Parliament over the degree to which it was able to impose conscription legislation upon the Manx people, further shifting authority away from the unelected lieutenant governor.

The spring of 1943 saw the culmination of the island's drive to gather scrap metal for the Ministry of Supply in the UK. The various local authorities had arranged dumping grounds, and asked people in their districts to deposit any unwanted metal that they might have there. When sufficient metal was collected, it was brought to Douglas and shipped to England. Appeals were made in particular to farmers and industrial firms for their help as they were the most likely to have quantities of heavy scrap material such as old ploughs. If anyone had scrap metal that was too heavy for them to bring to the dumping grounds, they could inform their local commissioners of its position and it was collected. To set an example, the iron railings surrounding the government offices in Douglas were removed and were sent away for scrap. Although the streets of Douglas generally avoided the wholesale destruction of railings outside private houses which took place in English

The Shore Garage in Port St Mary advises customers that it is 'carrying on', to use a wartime expression.

towns and cities, her churchyards did not get off so lightly. Ballure burial ground was denuded of its railings and more than 130 tons of metalwork was removed from graves in Kirk Braddan burial ground alone.

Scrap of a different kind was to be found on Douglas Head, where local schoolboy Toni Onley (later to become one of Canada's most famous artists) remembered:

> Perhaps because the island had not suffered from bombing, the war had produced in us such a fascination with explosives that I liked making bombs almost as much as I liked painting. We biked over to the artillery firing range on Douglas Head. The range closed on the weekends and [my friend] and I used to ride there often, sneak in and pick up unexploded trench mortar shells. We'd tie them to the handlebars of our bikes and ride back home. I shudder to think now what might have happened if an accident had banged the shells against the ground... We hammered the fins off the mortar shells, unscrewed the nose cones and emptied the cordite into lead pipes. We drilled a little touch hole in the bottom of each pipe, then attached a fuse.[1]

These schoolboy bomb-makers were only a couple of years younger than many of the servicemen and women who were training on the island in preparation for real combat. In order to assist the trainee RAF air gunners, a futuristic facility was constructed in the grounds of the Villa Marina. The Dome Trainer was a pod-shaped structure inside which a projector and an ingenious arrangement of mirrors beamed up an image of an attacking aircraft onto the curved ceiling. The trainee stood behind the projector with a dummy Browning machine gun and 'fired' at the target along with realistic sound effects. An instructor could measure the accuracy of the shooter by the presence of yellow lights projected onto the interior of the dome.

Intensive wireless training also took place, and that spring an ATS recruit named Thora Hindle was posted to the Isle of Man for this purpose. By that time, the Japanese internees, who Frank Cowin recalled as having red circles on their backs for identification purposes, had been moved away but Thora remembered that they had left numerous calling cards:

We disembarked on the quay in Douglas. This was my first visit to the Isle of Man. To demonstrate our marching skills we had learned in the small setting of [our previous] camp we marched along the promenade carrying kit bags, tin hats & gas masks & all wearing our heavy greatcoats. We passed a naval training unit, the *Valkyrie*. I seem to remember the unit was billeted in a large hotel now commandeered by the War Office for the duration. On we marched, arriving finally at a group of buildings encased by a heavy-duty wire fence making it into a secure compound. Everything appeared dull and grey. Eventually we shuffled off in small groups into various buildings (seafront hotels in peacetime). I was to be billeted in 'Homefield' [in] a small room at the front on the first floor to be shared with another ATS girl. 'What a dump' – we soon discovered that we had inherited the compound which had housed Japanese internees. The hotels had been vandalised by these male internees who had etched or gouged out the 'Rising Sun' on every flat surface available. Just everything was chipped & marked. The large mirrors which reflected the light in the dining room of the hotels (which were built close to high cliffs) were badly mutilated. This compound was to be 'home' and training school from spring through to autumn in 1943.

We were to be taught the Morse code – it proved to be quite a feat of high concentration in order to reach the high speeds required. In due course we were told that we were to be 'Intercept Operators' allocated to Interceptor Stations around the UK. Discretion was the watchword and we were not to talk about our training for special duties. For light relief we did PT & drill on the sands & the promenade. Our drill sergeant Sillitoe was an old soldier who revelled in army discipline – he encouraged us by telling us we were better than the *Valkyrie* sailors (I'm not sure we were so good!). The food on camp (cooked in basement kitchens) was uninteresting and two days a week we had to have 'ships' biscuits' to economise on the bread ration. [In] off-duty periods we escaped to Douglas town, the cinema & the wonderful canteens where 'egg & chips' was readily available. Swiss Cottage – a café nearer to Onchan Head – provided hot drinks and custard tarts, when we had money to spend on such goodies.[2]

The other common off-duty recreation was visiting the homes of local friends, and Thora remembered that the young service personnel were always made welcome by Manx families (whose own sons and daughters were perhaps serving overseas). All good things must end, however, and by late summer with training completed, these ATS girls were posted away. Some idea of the

The frontispiece of an Italian prayer book, published by priests for use in internment camps on the Isle of Man. The illustration, which shows St Anthony's Catholic Church in Onchan behind a barbed-wire fence, was drawn by Giuseppe Sorgiani, a well-known internee artist.

importance of the work for which they trained comes from the fact that messages received by Thora's intercept station were passed directly to Bletchley Park for decoding. However, the status and role of young women in the war was to become an increasing bone of contention between London and Douglas. In July 1943, a minor political earthquake took place, which afterwards would be identified as a milestone in the road to Manx political independence. After lengthy correspondence between Tynwald and the Home Office over respective differences in conscription and national service legislation, the House of Keys made its position clear to the Westminster government (and to its representative the lieutenant governor) that it was not prepared to extend legislation to the Isle of Man that would result in Manx women being compulsorily called up and sent away to England on war work.

In making this stand – in defiance of the wishes of Lord Granville – the Keys stated that they were acting in concord with public opinion, as evidenced by several recent by-elections, the successful candidates in which had all adopted this position. The Keys stated that the difficulties for young single Manx women working in the UK in getting to and from their homes were far greater than for those in England, Scotland or Wales. They added that they had no desire to stop women leaving voluntarily for war work; indeed, many had done so. It was a remarkable stance and was warmly applauded in the local press.

Yet as more and more young Manx men were called to the colours, labour on farms was in short supply. Much of the void was filled by working parties from the internment camps, and in many cases friendships and even relationships developed between the Manx families and the Italians sent to work with them. The farmers were for the most part pleased with the help, and the Italians glad of the opportunity to escape from the confines (and boredom) of the camps. The prospect of meeting young Manx women was an added bonus. Count Nikolai Giovannelli tells us of one party, and the story may well be autobiographical:

> The same three men continued to go to Ballamoar daily for several months, and became on very easy terms with both the Quayle family and their various guards, who were quite pleased to relax and enjoy a spot of leisure, knowing

that their prisoners were under supervision and working happily.

Often the guard would leave his gun outside the house and sit by the fire talking to Mrs Quayle, who was rather nervous of firearms, and if the motorbike of the inspecting Sergeant was heard coming along the farm road, one of the prisoners would rush in with the gun, push it into the guard's hand and say, '*Il Sargenti arriva*', so that all was in order when the inspection actually took place.

Mrs Quayle, in fact, almost mothered guards and prisoners alike, and began to speak of the three Italians as 'our boys', while over the midday meal many a friendly discussion took place about the war and the prospects of the end being not so far away.

The prisoners began to bring to their kind hosts small presents contrived with much trouble and effort in their restricted conditions at the camp, such as a string bag or a ship in a bottle made for Mrs Quayle, a handwoven belt or a monogram carved in bone for Fenella, and a silver-mounted walking stick and silver signet ring bearing his initials for Mr Quayle.[3]

If the camp authorities knew about this fraternization, they took little notice of it so long as it remained harmless and eased the tension at a difficult time for the prisoners. The tolerant attitude of the British was remarked upon by many Italians in later years. It was said that in the 1960s in London, if the proprietor of an Italian restaurant found out that a diner was from the Isle of Man they either got a good meal or (more rarely) shown the door, depending upon the owner's experiences of internment twenty years earlier!

Corporal Robert Quayle of Maughold had a different opinion of the Italians he encountered when in May his unit (the 1st Battalion, Parachute Regiment) landed in Tunisia. They were part of the Allied forces closing in on Rommel from the west:

Only a few days after landing in this country, I was in the front line. I was lucky to be put in a section of men who had been in action before. I'll never forget that first night, Jerry was attacking with all he had and we were put in to stop the gap... On another move it was our turn to attack, and we were taking on a hill called 'Sugar Loaf', because of its shape. To get to the hill we had to cross a river by a narrow pontoon bridge – of course it was my luck to slip and fall in, but my mates 'yanked' me out half-drowned. It wouldn't have been so bad only Jerry was just a few yards off.

We are a cheeky crowd. Going into the attack, we carried picks and shovels ready to dig in on top. It shows we had never thought of failure. When we were halfway up, Jerry's machine guns opened up almost straight away. I got a nick on the little finger of the left hand, but it was only a scratch. You should have seen the boys in the moonlight silhouetted against the skyline, going into a charge yelling the battle-cry 'Werho Mohammed' – that's a cry that puts the fear of death into any German. A week or two later we started the big attack that was to be the last. What a stroke of luck we had; the Jerry rearguards were Italians. You can tell what fighters they are. I roped in a bunch of 50 myself. As I handed them over, each one shook hands with me and kissed me on both cheeks! They were sure glad to be out of it all. One of them could speak a little English, and came up and threw his arms around my neck shouting, 'My saviour, my rescuer.' The boys nearly died laughing.

It was surprising the number of white handkerchiefs they had, brand new, some still wrapped in cellophane paper. We pushed the enemy back past Sedjenare when we were going in for the kill (Bizerta)…the paratroops bought every inch of the ground and paid plenty for it. Since we have been out of the line we have been complimented by various Generals on our 'magnificent work'. But the Germans, who are without a doubt the best soldiers in the world (bar us, of course), paid us the biggest compliment of all when they called us 'The Red Devils'.[4]

In July 1943 Quayle took part in Operation HUSKY, the Allied invasion of Sicily. In the same operation was another young Manx man, Mr Douglas J.H. Hardy, ARPS, a British naval war photographer who captured some fine pictures of what was up to that point the greatest seaborne invasion in history. The 28-year-old Hardy was an old boy of the Douglas High School, and after leaving went to Manchester University where he took a science

A British Sherman tank, knocked out in the invasion of Sicily, rests forlornly by the side of the road. A few yards away stands a German 88mm anti-aircraft gun. (Library of Congress)

course. Later he became a freelance film cameraman working for independent film-producing companies, and specialized in documentary films. He wrote home:

> We landed here (Sicily) at an unearthly hour this morning with no more resistance than a few bursts of tracer. If the rest of the war is like this, it would be a walk-over. We waded ashore from the landing-craft, and fortunately did not get too wet. By daybreak there were prisoners coming in; they were a sorry-looking crowd. 'Musso' seems to be very unpopular. I worked until about eleven, and then had a swim, as there was nothing to do at the moment. Have

only seen two Jerry aircraft, and cannot understand it. They were all asleep when we came. Actually, I was the first war correspondent to land from a ship by a long way, thanks to being 'organised in true naval fashion'.[5]

Also present was Kirk Michael man Sapper Noel Caley, for whom the greatest inconvenience was the fact that cigarettes were virtually unobtainable there. Towards the end of the year, Caley would be hospitalized with malaria. He was a regular reader of the *Isle of Man Examiner* while on active service; indeed, he wrote to his parents that its arrival was always a 'red letter day'. Through its columns, Manx service personnel were able to keep up with news of what friends and neighbours were doing while on active service, as well as with news from home. By the same token, readers at home kept up with what their soldier sons and brothers had been doing abroad.

Kirk Michael man Sapper Noel Caley, Royal Engineers, who took part in the invasion of Sicily. (Courtesy of John Caley)

For example, some months later the newspaper reported in detail on Tynwald Day which was celebrated by the Manx Regiment at Homs in Libya, and though it was impossible to observe 'the Fair' on the actual day owing to the regiment being engaged on combined operations exercises, the opportunity was taken to observe the island's national day on the third Sunday in July. A special church parade was followed in the afternoon by regimental sports. The Reverend Gordon Sayle, Manx chaplain to the regiment, conducted the service and he also arranged to have a Manx choir assembled. Through careful husbandry of the beer ration by some soldiers prior to the day itself, plus the acquisition of some local brandy by the battery sergeant majors, thirsts were amply quenched in the evening, while the Manxmen were kept busy explaining to the non-Manx members of the regiment what all this Tynwald Day was about! Nobly the non-Manx members refused to let their 'ignorance' interfere with their enjoyment.

The landing in Sicily hastened the fall of Mussolini and the Fascist government in Rome, a development that would have far-reaching implications for the Italians interned on the Isle of Man. In the short term, however, it brought to the fore once again tensions between pro-Fascist and anti-Fascist Italians on the island. Count Nikolai Giovannelli remembered:

> On July 26th as we were marching to Derby Castle station to board the electric car which took us to our allotted work, a Douglas resident passing our party on his bicycle called out, 'Mussolini is out! Mussolini is out!' We looked at each other, and of course began to discuss this momentous information among ourselves.
>
> 'This looks like the beginning of the end,' I whispered to Gabrielli, and he agreed: 'Yes Nick, we've got what we asked for.' But we had no further information until we got back to the camp that evening where we found pandemonium and all kinds of speculation going around. At eight o'clock the Military Commander asked the whole camp to listen to a special bulletin which went more or less like this: 'The Italian King and Grand Consiglio have dismissed Mussolini and abrogated his Government. Marshal Badoglio is to form a new Government and start talks with the Allies, Signor R. Quariglia is elected Foreign Minister. Marshal De Bono is arrested and Mussolini imprisoned in the Grand Sasso in Abruzzi.'
>
> There was another uproar after that, and a few heads were broken, but shortly we managed to calm down most of it. Next day we went out to work as usual, and listened to the radio for some foreign bulletin which might give us a better view of the situation, but they all confirmed the BBC one. That night the council was asked to meet, and my greeting from them was, 'Well, bastard, your wish has come true, eh?'[6]

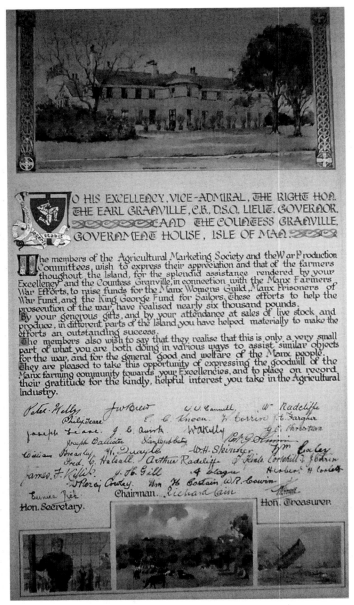

This illuminated address, designed by John H. Nicholson, conveyed the gratitude of the Agricultural Marketing Society for the help given to their war effort by Lord and Lady Granville. It features an illustration of Government House, the hub of much illicit wartime trading. (Courtesy of Manx National Heritage)

A few months later, with the armistice in Italy signed, many Italians began to drift away, with some being repatriated to their home country. Only a rump remained on the island until 1945.

If food was restricted on the Isle of Man, it was still generally speaking in more plentiful supply than in most parts of the United Kingdom. It was whispered that one of the main hubs for contraband in and out of the island was actually Government House, and there were claims that sides of pork and sacks of flour were frequently dropped off there, en route to England with Lord Granville. With his contacts in the Royal Navy, the lieutenant governor was also able to obtain bananas from West Africa, which came back via destroyer to Liverpool and thence on to the Isle of Man.

Unlike bananas, which were unobtainable for most ordinary people on the island, fish was readily available. However, newspapers urged the Manx government to take charge of the herring industry in Peel, where in recent weeks there had been chaotic scenes. Differences in herring catches had seen first a glut and then a shortage of fish, with prices fluctuating wildly. The big problem for the buyers this year had been labour. Most of the kipper-curers could have dealt with larger quantities of herring each day had they larger staffs. A kipper-curer could only manage with a percentage of unskilled labour, and skilled labour that summer was almost unobtainable due to the war. A few local kipper merchants had invested in herring-splitting machines, but another grouse among the local and some regular Scottish crews at Peel concerned ring-net fishermen from the Clyde. They had arrived in the port in recent weeks, and because of their method of fishing could land their herrings earlier than the drift-net boats that worked according to the sun and not the clock. On several occasions when the drift-net boats came into harbour the 'ringers' had already sold their catches to the kipper merchants. Naturally the merchants could not purchase the Manx catch as well, and the fish were sold off cheap. Newspapers argued that there should be no gambling in a market for foodstuffs in wartime, and that with millions of people in the world who would be glad of salted herrings (the Russians, for instance), every fish it was possible to catch should be landed and cured for shipment to wherever they might be required. If the Manx government had made better arrangements to manage the curing of the fish and better co-

The night fishing permit issued by the naval officer in charge at Douglas to William Radcliffe, at one time admiral of the herring fleet. Under the Defence of the Realm Act, Manx waters were restricted. (Courtesy of Manx National Heritage)

ordinate the two parts of the industry, many more herring might have been exported.

The herring fishery had always employed many women, and the difficulties it was experiencing were in no small part due to the fact that these women were now largely working in munitions factories or on the land. As in many other wars there were widespread concerns, particularly among churchmen, that soldiers on leave, alcohol and young women away from home were a bad combination and would lead to an increase in vice. In its Christmas edition, however, the *Isle of Man Times*, while repeating this message parrot-fashion, was also forced to admit that the island had not been seriously affected in this way: '...our inquiries from medical men and the officials of the Local Government Board lead us to believe that there is no evident local increase in venereal disease, and the pursuit of our own profession leaves us unaware of any increase in the conviction for drunkenness or indecency.'[7]

By the end of the year, hopes were beginning to rise that the following twelve months might actually see the conclusion of the conflict. In closing a letter to his family, Charlie McGovern (pre-war stage manager for the Legion Players and the Student Players, and at the time serving with the RAF in North Africa), wrote: 'All good wishes for 1944 Victory Year, and here's to the day when old Douglas Head is no longer a mirage, but a reality.'[8]

Such hopes, however, were optimistic. Even though the Western Allies had agreed to devote all their efforts to the defeat of Germany before fully turning their attention to Japan, Hitler's 'Fortress Europe' would still prove to be a far harder nut to crack than many imagined. The coming year would see the longed-for second front opened up in the West, but the resistance of the two remaining Axis powers would drag the war out for almost a full eighteen months more. On the island, the important work of training men and women for war continued, and 1943 had perhaps seen the first signs of a growing sense of awareness and self-confidence in the House of Keys as a result.

CHAPTER SIX

1944: The Highest Courage

By the beginning of 1944, the direction of the war had clearly turned in favour of the Allies. On the home front, Mr J.R. Quayle of the Isle of Man Bank summarized the island's position at the annual general meeting of shareholders. The visiting industry was still largely in abeyance, though the amount of English money that had passed over the counters in branches the previous summer was higher than that of the year before, suggesting that holidaymakers were slowly returning. All the main products of agriculture were controlled at prices which, though they offered a fair return for the management and labour expended, did not permit high profits. The greatest problem was the supply of labour, and it was to the credit of the farmers that they had responded so loyally to demands for increased food production. The fishing industry was in the main confined to Peel, though catches were good and monetary turnover higher than the previous year. The bulk of the herring was landed by Scottish and Irish boats.

On the battlefield, the Germans had been driven out of North Africa, but the war in Italy was locked in stalemate. The Allied advance along the mountainous backbone of the country had been held up at Monte Cassino, where a determined German defence of the monastery overlooking the main north-south highway held them in check. The Anzio landing in January 1944 was conceived as a means of outflanking the defenders, but this too became bogged down. A stretcher-bearer, Private William Faragher of Ballacubbon, St Marks took part in the landing with the Loyal North Lancashire Regiment; indeed, he was in one of the first waves of troops ashore at Anzio. Private Faragher was out six or seven times a day with his stretcher, for weeks on end. On one occasion, he was on duty with a company of his battalion in action near a position known as Fly-over-Bridge. A neighbouring battalion's detachment had lost many of its men as well as all its officers, and its own stretcher-bearers were unable to reach the wounded. Private Faragher volunteered to go forward and bring in the other unit's casualties, a task that he carried out with great success. Later, in the battles of the Gothic Line, he went out as a member of a stretcher-bearer party in the face of a German counter-attack and again brought in a number of injured men. This time he was severely wounded himself by machine-gun fire and was in hospital for four months. Not surprisingly, Faragher was awarded the Military Medal for his bravery during the Anzio campaign.

Back on the Isle of Man, the island's role as an instructional and training centre continued unabated. At RAF Andreas, the fighter station established to the north of Ramsey, there had been a lull in operations since the departure of 93 Squadron about a year earlier, but the spring of 1944 saw an increase in activity once more as No. 11 Air Gunners' School arrived to take up residence. This unit had formed in the previous year to give instruction to air gunners over the Irish Sea (in conditions of relative safety), initially using Avro Ansons and Miles Martinets before gradually dropping the latter type and also flying some Supermarine Spitfires and Vickers Wellingtons. As it was constructed during the war itself, Andreas was a simpler and more basic airfield than its counterpart at Jurby. A number of its buildings survive however, most notably the station cinema which today serves as Andreas village hall.

Naval recruits continued to be trained at HMS *St George* in Douglas, as one of the trainees, Frank Bowen, recounts. Bowen was from Liverpool and had volunteered at the recruiting office there for service as a boy entrant into the Royal Navy. Although he had signed the necessary paperwork, he could not join until his sixteenth birthday, which came in March 1944. Shortly after this he was in naval uniform on a ferry, escorted by a destroyer, to the Isle of Man:

> I went in as a trainee wireless operator...we called them telegraphists...and I went into a class and there was wireless operators coming up type of thing. You did four weeks

of what they called Nozzers [new Royal Navy entrant] training where you were taught to march, hold a rifle, shoot it, all the things for learning to toe the line and look like someone who knew what he was doing. So that was about it. After the basic month, you left what they called Nozzers and joined your class, and you started education. And we spent half of the day in classrooms and there, we used to march to a place called the Ballakermeen High School, which was converted to a military base. And then we spent four hours of the day there on schooling and then four hours of the day learning to be wireless operators and marching, seamanship, everything that was involved with the service. And that was really about it. The course, the seaman's course, took six months to put a seaman boy to go to sea. And it took a year and a half on average for a wireless operator. And this was cut down in places. Mine was cut short because I did quite well in my educational side of it.[1]

The base also encompassed Cunningham's Camp on Victoria Road, with part of the establishment on either side of the road linked by a tunnel. A large mast carried the white ensign, while at the northern edge underground bomb shelters were constructed. These may well have also been used for smoke training. Much of this accommodation of course had previously been used by the visiting industry, and thoughts were now beginning to turn to what form the sector should take after the war was over. Much of the accommodation had been damaged by military use, but even that which had not would need to be upgraded if the island were to attract visitors once more. The *Isle of Man Examiner* argued that those involved in the tourist trade had previously been much too modest in putting forward any claim for assistance, despite their importance to the economy of the island. It continued:

There are many directions in which the visiting industry requires to be modernised – this despite the many advances made during the years preceding the war – and when we return to the days of intensified competition between the resorts, we will fall behind in the race unless all our hotels and boarding houses are in every way comparable

Boy recruits at HMS St George, the Royal Navy training school established in the chalets of the Douglas Holiday Camp on Victoria Road. (Author's collection)

with those in other places. To achieve this will mean the expenditure of a good deal of capital – probably more than even the most prosperous of our boarding-house-keepers can afford – and here is one direction in which Government assistance should be available on reasonable terms.[2]

Frank Cowin's family ran one such guest house in Douglas, but he remembered:

We were one of the few boarding houses [on the Promenade] that was still open, and of course we were busy. It was unlike the First World War situation where the trade just disappeared...some of the visitors were relatives of people who were here – relatives of those who were training here, or who were interned here, because very often it would only be father who was interned, and the rest of the family, mother and the children were not, so we stayed open. Of course then there was all this kerfuffle of how long were they staying, did they need to bring their ration books and surrender them, did they bring the likes of eggs with them, if they did, they had their name written on them, and expected to get their own egg back when they had it! As I understand it we got extra coupons because of the people who were staying, so there was extra food available.[3]

Other food was within reach of the Manx, particularly if they had access to relatives in the countryside:

There were lots of connections with farmers, and my memories of many of the summer holidays were of going out to a farm in the Ballaugh area where I would go with my grandmother. They had a stall at the market and came in every week and we used to go down there to get stuff from them...but every so often in the summer we would take a day out on the train, grandma and myself, and maybe a brother...and we'd spend the day on the farm, and we'd go home with all sorts of goodies, including Manx butter![4]

The War Provisions Bill (and other legislation relating to agriculture) gave the Manx government great powers over farmers. They could instruct them on what to grow, could take over control of land that was not being used productively and even hand the running of farms to other tenants if they were not being worked efficiently. Some insight into how the war affected small farmers comes from Adrian Wall, who owned land at Cardle Veg in the north of the island. He wrote in his semi-autobiographical *Cardles Farm Once More*:

Looking back, I wish I had started farming years before, as the war period brought so many difficulties and disturbances; one was worried by changes caused by different conditions, irritating rules and regulations, made without the decree of Parliament and, in many cases, without any notice to those engaged in farming. Then the sheaves of forms and the petty pinpricks which could have been avoided if those on the Civil Service stools had had some practical knowledge and experience.

Our men had not been taught book-keeping, either double- or single-entry, and I should not be far wrong if I said the only forms they had filled up were their football coupons, and possibly a piece of paper giving the name of a horse, with the stake on it as the token of hope that it would win the Derby or some minor race.

Never, even by accident, did the forms balance, as John could not understand that the number of cattle on the farm on the 1st January, plus cattle bought or born during the year, deducting the cattle which were sold, or had died, during the same time, should equal the cattle on the farm on the 31st December; never could John arrive at the right balance, and one year when I pointed out to him that the figures didn't agree, his reply was, 'They never have, but nothin' happens!'[5]

Arguably the most isolated of all Manx farms was not even on the Isle of Man: Carey's farm on the Calf of Man was operated by R.B. Mitchell, the Calf Warden. For much of the time, when weather was bad, the tiny island was entirely cut off, but in the summer of 1944 in an extraordinary operation, Mitchell had a Fordson tractor delivered by E.B. Christian, the island's main Ford dealer. The tractor was broken down into its components and taken across the Sound in two boats, then reassembled on the Calf. Christian and his team had taken enough tinned food for three days in case they were cut off by bad weather, but in the event they were able to return on the next tide. The Fordson was the workhorse of Britain's agricultural war effort, and many thousands were produced at the Dagenham factory. Possibly Mitchell had acquired a war surplus example, but this was the first attempt at mechanized farming on the Calf of Man, and perhaps Mitchell was attempting to make the farm pay its way in straitened wartime conditions.

By now momentum was gathering for an even greater amphibious operation: the Allied invasion of France and the opening-up of the so-called 'second front'. Manx people had an early foretaste of what was happening, as some of the convoys that would take part in the landings formed up off the Isle of Man, and indeed some of the landing craft waited in Douglas harbour for other ships to arrive. Just as they had done at Dunkirk, the vessels

Eric Cain who, as a young galley-hand, took part in the D-Day landings aboard SS Ben-my-Chree *in June 1944. Like most of the Merchant Navy crew, he was trained to operate anti-aircraft weapons as well. (Courtesy of Sarah Clucas)*

of the Isle of Man Steam Packet Company would play a key role in the coming landings. However, one of the ships, SS *Viking*, almost did not make it, having a number of narrow escapes from Hitler's V-1 rockets which were becoming an increasing problem in southern England at the time. Captain A. Holkham remembered later:

When we went to the Thames to take part in D-Day, while at anchor the *Viking* had a very narrow escape. A flying bomb dropped about 90 feet away causing extensive damage. The same thing happened while we were in dock for repairs. Finally she undertook the job of carrying troops to the Normandy beaches, which was a picnic compared to what we had had to put up with during the flying bombs.[6]

At this time Douglas-born Eric Cain was a 17-year-old Merchant Navy sailor, recently passed out from the training ship *Vindicatrix* as a galley-hand. He went into the Merchant Navy 'pool' and was posted to his first ship in Liverpool. This lasted only two days, however, before she hit an obstruction. His next posting was to an unnamed ship at Gourock on the Clyde. Upon arrival at the port he was surprised to find that his new vessel was the *Ben-my-Chree*. At that time, something like 70 per cent of the crew was Manx with a smattering of English sailors, mainly from Liverpool. As well as having the advantage of being surrounded by familiar names, the situation also had its disadvantages. The second steward lived around the corner from Cain in Douglas, and told him to behave himself or he would soon tell his mother! The first trip was to South Shields to be modified for D-Day:

> We came out of the Clyde and there was a really top gale going on... We had to carry on, to go right up round the top of Scotland, and coming back down through the Pentlands we took a wave on the back end which took the entire back railings off and smashed the back open... Just one wave that went through. I remember standing where the galley was at the bottom of the staircase and seeing this complete block of water coming down the stairs and going right up into the big restaurant and it smashed everything up... We had to keep going, and we called into a small port and lay there about 24 hours, then the weather abated a bit and carried on to South Shields. The weather had already done half of what they were about to do in South Shields. They didn't need to strip the outer rail, it had been done! This was when they were going to convert it, for carrying landing barges. They were going to take off all the lifeboats and build it up to take six landing craft, the davits, but we didn't pick the barges up till we got down south.[7]

The ship was also heavily protected with defensive armaments, and even a technically civilian merchant sailor like Cain was expected to leave the galley and assist in the defence of the ship if she was attacked from the air:

> She had a double Oerlikon on each quarter, she had four of those double Oerlikons. After the funnel she had a Bofors manned by army gunners, and the Oerlikons were manned by Navy gunners. We were loaders, you were asked to load them. We never ever got round to banging them off properly, but you were trained on it, you took your part in it, in case someone got hurt, and there was an attack, you took your part in it... They had onboard two tramlines welded together and you put a rocket in the middle of it and fired it, and it was attached to a reel of very thin piano wire. The idea was that the rocket went up, pulled the roll of piano wire up, and then when it opened up a small parachute came out and held it long enough that it

slowly sank back down. The idea was that if any aircraft came along it would snag on the wings. So we decided to try it out but it didn't work, it came back down on the deck and got tangled up![8]

Although the ship was preparing for D-Day, the details of the Normandy landings were a well-kept secret; the only clue as to the *Ben*'s destination came from the fact that rather than practising landing troops on beaches, they repeatedly landed parties of US Rangers in barges against sheer cliffs, which the soldiers scaled with ladders. The reason for this became clear on D-Day itself, when the *Ben* landed troops at Pointe du Hoc, between Utah and Omaha beaches. Cain remembered:

We were about ten miles off shore...the weather was rough. They announced at the time that if we couldn't get the barges down and in the water, they would put the ship ashore. The entire ship was going to go ashore, and we would have to fend for ourselves. This came over the tannoy, from the captain, Duggan... The first barge we put down didn't have any soldiers in, they put it down to see if it could take the waves, because if it didn't they would put the entire ship ashore. Whether it would have survived getting through the mines we didn't know, because there were a lot of obstructions in the water... It was very well organised all round really. There was a big warship alongside us, and she was firing salvo after salvo, and you could hear these one-ton shells she was firing, going through the air. They were hissing as they went through the air... I was on watch on deck and could see all this happening.[9]

Duggan was a skilful captain. Having lowered his barges on the lee side, when the heavy swell prevented him from lowering those on the windward side, he swung the ship around and used it to protect them. The Rangers had become friendly with the Manx crew during the time they had been aboard, often passing on American candy and other luxuries. One in particular gave Cain his address in the Bronx and asked him to look him up if he ever made it to New York. This he did on a transatlantic posting after the war,

One of the D-Day invasion beaches, crowded with landing craft. The Ben-my-Chree *may be among those further out to sea, having launched her barges containing US Rangers. (Library of Congress)*

only to find from the man's distraught mother that his friend had later been killed in Normandy.

Hector Duff meanwhile had returned from Italy to prepare for D-Day. All the heavy equipment had been left behind in Italy and the unit had been re-equipped with Cromwell tanks, with which the men had to familiarize themselves. They were fully aware of what they were preparing for. Hector was put into an armoured car squadron, and was to escort the brigadier on D-Day. At Felixstowe they loaded onto landing craft, but their destination was still a mystery. After several days of seasickness in the Channel aboard the flat-bottomed craft, the brigadier opened his orders.

> When we got within four or five miles in towards France we could hear the shelling, and our planes going over. Fortunately there weren't many Luftwaffe about, but our planes were going, and ships were coming back. But we

Hector Duff in Europe during 1944. He was wounded during the break-out from the Normandy bridgehead, when his tank was hit by enemy fire. (Courtesy of Hector Duff)

couldn't see very much of it because we were down below the gunnel of the ship. Once we got a bit nearer the skipper of the boat said now start up your engines, get them warmed up so they won't cut out or stall when you go into the water. And it was only then that we got up and we could see the extent of the horizon in front of us and there were boats of all shapes and sizes. We could see as we got closer there were shells landing in the water where we'd got to go. Then we realised it was a terrific operation, as we got closer of course it dawned on us what it was like, we were being shelled...boats were being hit as we got closer but not an awful lot. This was about 2 o'clock, and a lot of the enemy artillery had been pushed back. As we got closer in we could see all the obstacles on the beaches. When the first troops landed in the morning the tide was in and covered it, but when we landed the tide had come out and we could see them, so the skipper had a chance of weaving in and out and through. There were an awful lot of smaller boats that had been hit and had been sunk or were burning, and he did have a bit of a difficult job but he got in and we landed in about two foot of water and the ramp went down... There was all sorts of carnage of war, our vehicles, jeeps and a lot of Bren gun carriers, and an awful lot of German gun positions that had been overrun. And hundreds of bodies, literally, in the sea and all the way, hundreds of bodies everywhere.[10]

Later on during the Normandy campaign, Duff took part in the battles of Goodwood and Epsom, as the British armoured forces attempted to break out of the Normandy bridgehead, before being wounded when his tank was hit.

While the war against the Germans was being waged in the West, preparations were also beginning for the final phase of the campaign against Japan. Across the great expanses of the Pacific Ocean, battles could be fought between fleets which never actually saw each other, the combat being conducted through air power. In this campaign, aircraft carriers would be the key to success and although the great carrier fleets of the US navy are associated with battles such as Midway and Leyte Gulf, the British Pacific Fleet also took a prominent role. Here again, the Isle of

Sergeant George Cleator, 2nd Battalion, Cheshire Regiment, of Ramsey. He was awarded the Military Medal for an action in Normandy in June 1944 when a German counter-attack was fought off by his platoon. (Courtesy of Bev Lord)

Man would play a part in training air-crew for the campaign. The departure of the RAF from Ronaldsway was a key event, as it allowed the Admiralty to move into the airfield, massively transforming the place. Among other infrastructure improvements came hard runways and additional hangars. Many of these items are still readily evident today and, as an incidental point, the extension work revealed more of the archaeological evidence that was already known to exist at Ronaldsway and established beyond all doubt that the Neolithic culture that had existed on the island was unique. Unlike most airfields constructed during the Second World War (including Andreas), which conformed to the standard RAF three-runway pattern, Ronaldsway had four runways to comply with Admiralty requirements; crosswinds were not a problem on aircraft carriers and so there had to be more choices of 'into wind' runway. The runways were also narrower than the standard 50 yards, because in order to simulate aircraft carrier deck landings they were only 30 yards wide. Post-war this would result in considerable work to widen two of them to civil aviation standards. HMS *Urley*, as the the base was known, came into being officially on 21 June 1944 and had as its main task torpedo bomber reconnaissance and associated training.

The first Fleet Air Arm unit, 747 Naval Air Squadron, arrived on 14 July 1944 equipped with Fairey Barracuda II aircraft, followed by 713 Naval Air Squadron on 12 August, also with Barracuda IIs. The final Barracuda squadron, 710 Naval Air Squadron, reformed at Ronaldsway on 7 October. It was equipped with Barracuda II and III aeroplanes, and also operated the Fairey Swordfish biplane. The three permanently-based squadrons had altogether 92 Barracudas between them out of a total of 120 naval aircraft based at Ronaldsway. There were also several temporary detachments of squadrons to HMS *Urley*, including four Miles Martinets from 725 Naval Air Squadron based there between August and November to provide air-to-air firing facilities.

Joan Roylance was a 20-year-old WREN when in 1944 she was posted to Ronaldsway as a Fleet Air Arm air mechanic. She never regretted her experience during the war, describing it as her university, and having gone into the navy as a shy schoolgirl she discovered that she had many talents and capabilities that stood her in good stead in later life. Joan was based at Ballasalla Camp in Nissen huts, known in naval parlance as cabins. Each WREN cabin contained twelve bunks, and was under the supervision of a petty officer. A wire fence separated the womens' part of the camp from that of the male ratings. There was, however, some fraternization along the fence, particularly when the rum ration was issued, to male personnel only. Each morning the WRENs marched down to the airfield, where Joan worked on air frames. She remembered:

> We repaired wings and surfaces, and the great big oleo legs, and perspex, if that had been damaged we'd put in new pieces. There was rather a lot of riveting. I came in very useful because I was the only WREN working with

Naval personnel at HMS Urley, Ronaldsway, in 1944. The men are likely to be engine-fitters and airframe mechanics. (Courtesy of Dawn Beck)

the men, and I'd got a very small hand, so when you were doing riveting my little hand went in the small gaps when the men couldn't get theirs in...

We used to repair them if they were damaged, mostly Barracudas, which didn't have a very happy life, because it was night training and they had rather a lot of crashes, and we sometimes had to go out and pick up the bits, which was not very nice. The Barracudas had a bad reputation, but then we got Grumman Martlets in, which were American planes. We had to have a supply store in the hangar with all the tools that we needed, and a lot of American equipment came over.

I didn't come across the officers very much, they were mostly the pilots. Occasionally we'd see them – some of the girls did, but I didn't. I was a bit young, I hadn't ever been in a pub and didn't drink, but the men used to of course. I had my bike, and we used to go down to Port St Mary swimming, and we used to cycle to Port Erin to go to the cinema, and we used to meet up with the Italian prisoners of war... We met them in cafés and in the cinema, and talked to them.[11]

By this stage in the war, with Italy now a co-belligerent, there was a much more relaxed attitude on the part of the authorities towards those Italians who remained on the island. Indeed, with many of them working in agriculture they were seen as a valuable help and were allowed to move around freely. A similarly relaxed attitude seems to have been the norm at Rushen Camp at this time. In one incident that took place on a late June evening in 1944 two girls named Elisabeth Huber and Thea Bayerl were seen by WPC 158 Florence Hillary getting through the wire that formed part of the boundary of the women's internment camp. They climbed an earth bank (about 5ft in height) and pulled the strands of the wire apart and got through into the adjoining field. When questioned, they both said that they were just picking flowers. They then returned through the wire without further repercussions.

By contrast, from the summer of 1944 onwards, Hutchinson Camp, now cleared of internees, was home to German military prisoners captured on the Normandy battlefields. Gone was the gnome-like studiousness and sense of bookish academia that had characterized Hutchinson in earlier years, to be replaced with an air of arrogance and menace. Leather-coated officers paced inside the wire like caged animals; on at least one occasion sexual remarks were made towards a teenage girl on her way home past the wire (remarks which were not repeated when she

WREN Joan Roylance of Leeds, who was stationed at HMS Urley. (Courtesy of Dawn Beck)

returned with her father, a camp guard with a loaded rifle). The gradual release of internees also freed up accommodation for other purposes, and the Isle of Man was used as a reception centre for those who had managed to escape from occupied Europe in order to debrief them and vet them to eliminate possible quislings or enemy agents.

One of these was a young Norwegian named Reidar Drengsrud. Despite some misgivings about leaving behind his mother and two sisters, he managed to slip away from the German work party to which he had been assigned and made his way to neutral Sweden. Here Norwegian forces in exile received him and, when told of his wish to join the Royal Norwegian Air Force, prepared him with some initial training. In August 1944 a secret flight took him to RAF Leuchars in Scotland. From here he takes up the story:

German prisoner of war Wili Adam, who was captured in Normandy in 1944 and held in Hutchinson camp. (Courtesy of Wili Adam)

> Eventually we reached our land of hope and expectation in a very good and friendly atmosphere. However, this atmosphere changed to the opposite as soon as our feet had touched British ground. Under guards we were marched away for a breakfast meal, then to a small transport plane. Without any information, we took off for the Isle of Man. After a few hours' flight we landed on an airfield... British guards carrying sticks marched us into a camp fenced by barbed wire. We learned that the name was Onchan, a camp for POWs and detainees and that our next future had to be spent on 'the Island of Barbed Wire'. That was a real blow.

With regard to the accommodation in the camp, I cannot remember how many we were in each room. The treatment was fairly good except that we were not allowed to leave the camp. Our time was shared between meals and interrogations by British officers. Later on in the stay we got the feeling that we in a way were privileged. Still together with our guards we were taken by bus around the island to various places associated with our common history during the Viking period. Very clever guides told us more of our history than any of us knew.

The stay in Onchan camp lasted for about one week, one Sunday included. That Sunday afternoon was very warm and we were marched down to the beach for a nice swim in the sea. Refreshed and in good spirits we stopped in a small square for a rest on our way back to the camp. Some people were gathered there enjoying like us the nice afternoon. We asked our guards if we could sing some Norwegian songs... Our wish was granted. We sang student songs, typical Norwegian songs and ended up with a song which at that time was about to become a new national hymn, *Norge i hvtt, rødt og blått*. People crowded around us and were told by the guards that we were patriots from Norway who had fled the country to join the free Norwegian forces in the UK. The return to the camp was a triumph and for the people who had followed us back, it seemed unbelievable when we were locked behind the barbed wire.[12]

After this, Drengsrud and his party left via steamer for Liverpool and then to a further interrogation centre near London before he succeeded in joining the Royal Norwegian Air Force. In later life he reflected upon the fact that the interrogation process and the stay on the Isle of Man was a vital security measure given the circumstances, and most of the Norwegians accepted this at the time. Recent research suggests that around 1,000 to 1,500 males escaped from occupied Norway between April and October 1944 with the intention of joining Allied forces; most of these were held in Onchan Camp for ten to fifteen days. Practically all came via Sweden, and had been brought to RAF Leuchars as part of Operation SONNIE, the escape route run by Norwegian patriot Bernt Balchen. HRH Crown Prince Olaf of Norway flew in to the Isle of Man on 6 September 1944 with the intention of meeting some of his countrymen who had escaped in this way.

By the late summer of 1944 the Allied advance in Western Europe was slowing. With their armies at the end of ever-lengthening supply lines, British and American generals found the process of driving back stubborn German forces growing increasingly difficult. At this point, Field Marshal Bernard Montgomery came up with a bold plan to end the war by Christmas. He proposed to drop a parachute army 30 miles behind German lines in Holland to capture a series of key bridges across the Rhine. This operation, code-named MARKET GARDEN, promised both to cut off German forces in The Netherlands and allow British and American armour directly into the industrial heartland of the Ruhr.

Crown Prince Olaf of Norway, who visited his compatriots held briefly on the Isle of Man. (Library of Congress)

In spite of the bravery of the men involved, the operation was a failure. One of those from the Isle of Man who participated was Major Robert Henry Cain of the 2nd Battalion, South Staffordshire Regiment. Cain had been born in Shanghai, of Manx parents. He recalled that he and his men were delayed by twenty-four hours, the tow rope on their Horsa glider having broken on their first attempt to join the battle:

> We had left in very filthy weather indeed, low cloud and rain, but after a while it improved... A little while after mid-Channel I saw the coastline of Holland in front. It was a buff-fawny colour, with white and grey streaks... The next thing I recognised was the Rhine. Then we got flak puffs all around us and bits of tracer. I got the fellows strapped

in. Geary put her into a dive approach. It seemed to be about treetop level when he pulled her out straight...and shouted 'Hold tight!' and we landed in a ploughed field. We got out and took up all-round protective positions... All the area was divided up into square fields with little tree-lined earth roads dividing them. It was very neat and very square. The trees were elms. I could hear very little firing, and what there was, was a long way off. There was no other activity. We moved off in the proper order of march, and I remember checking several men as they went past for things like not having their bayonets fixed. It was so like an exercise that I did this automatically.[13]

Fighting their way up towards Arnhem to join the main British force, Cain and his men eventually found their path blocked by superior German forces. Against tanks in particular, the lightly-armed British airborne troops had little with which to respond. He continued:

Up near the Museum we were under close attack from tanks – so close that our battalion mortars, using only the primary charges, fired almost vertically in their efforts to hit them. When a tank appeared we got four Brens firing on it with tracers. That shut its lid up because the commander couldn't stand up in the turret. As soon as we'd let off a PIAT at it, we'd move back and then the German shells would explode below us. It was impossible to tell how many tanks there were and I don't think we ever disabled one for we never saw the crew get out. At about 1130 the PIAT ammunition gave out. The tanks came up and our men were being killed one after the other. I saw one of our men with only his face left. His eyes were wide open. We could hear the call of 'stretcher-bearer' all the time. The German tanks blew up the house next to to us and set it on fire. There was nothing we could do about these beasts because we had no ammunition.[14]

For his efforts in the Arnhem campaign, Cain was to be decorated with the Victoria Cross. He remains the only Manx serviceman to have received the coveted award. The failure of MARKET GARDEN underlined just how difficult overcoming German resistance in the West was going to be. Being fully aware of how

Major Robert Henry Cain VC, who received the supreme award for bravery at Arnhem.

strong the temptation to desert or surrender to the British and American forces might be, they had deployed their most fanatical troops, with several battle-hardened SS divisions among them.

Casualties continued to mount and, just before Christmas 1944, a young wife received the worst possible news. Mrs E.M. Gale of 'Sea View', Mount Murray, Santon, who earlier had received word that her husband, Rifleman John James Gale, 2nd Battalion, Royal Ulster Rifles, was missing and believed to be a prisoner of war, now had official confirmation from Infantry Records that he had been killed in action on 30 November. Mrs Gale also received a letter from Major Edward Murphey, her husband's commanding officer, who asked her to feel pride and consolation in the fact that her husband died while performing his duty. Major Murphey continued:

> Your husband was one of those chosen to advance in the open against an enemy village. To do this takes men of stout heart and high courage, and your husband has proved himself to be one. He and the others who fell with him in

the action displayed the highest courage. Your husband was a good soldier and popular with his comrades.[15]

Rifleman Gale, who was buried in a Dutch village, left four young children, the eldest a boy of 13. It was further evidence that the freedom of Europe would come only at a great price in lives, and the Isle of Man contributed to that cost without hesitation. With the fifth anniversary of the outbreak of war just passed, Manx newspapers announced that the total number killed up to this point from the island itself stood at just over 400 (the North American Manx Association further informed readers that six Canadian and three American soldiers of Manx descent had also been killed thus far in the war.) Commentators added that terrible as it was, thankfully the figure was far below that suffered in the four years of the Great War. However, with hindsight it is easy to see that the military destruction of the German army, which was a necessary precursor for victory in both wars, was carried out largely by the British and French in the First World War, whereas in the second the task fell mainly to the Russians in the East, with similar results.

A Morris self-propelled Bofors gun of the Manx Regiment, somewhere in north-west Europe during the winter of 1944–45. (Courtesy of the Manx Aviation Preservation Society/Manx Regiment Museum)

CHAPTER SEVEN

1945: A Job Well Done

Despite the failure of the offensive at Arnhem the previous year, 1945 opened with a positive sense that the defeat of Nazi Germany could not be far away. On the Isle of Man the mood was more relaxed than it had been in earlier years, and security restrictions less severe than they had been at the beginning of the war. It was not long, however, before events conspired to show that the Germans were still capable of hitting back at Britain. In what was to be one of their last hurrahs, a wolf-pack of German U-boats succeeded in slipping through the approaches to the Bristol Channel and into the Irish Sea. On 15 January, the crew of a Dutch trawler fishing 3 miles off the Chicken Rock near the Calf of Man heard an explosion, and in the distance spotted a wall of flame some 200ft high. It was the fuel tanker *Maja*, defensively armed and with a mainly Chinese crew. The captain of the trawler made for the scene at once, guided by flares dropped by a Catalina flying boat, and amid the smoke and flames he could see the stern of a ship. It took them about an hour to reach the tanker. The trawler picked up a lifeboat in which were thirty-nine men, including the captain of the tanker, about 100 yards from the blazing ship. Patches of burning oil and wreckage were strewn over the sea. The tanker settled by the stern, and for a long time after they could see the forepart of the ship, red-hot, still above the water. The captain of the *Maja* said that he suspected they were the victims of a submarine attack. He had heard an explosion amidships, and at first thought they had struck a mine. The ship listed, but he thought he could make Liverpool. Later there were two more explosions in the benzine tanks.

An air-sea rescue launch from Douglas also went to the scene, skippered by Flying Officer Swanson. This was one of two such launches based in the harbour, and it would have reached the area rapidly. Following an earlier incident in which an aircraft had ditched outside the harbour but neither launch could leave its cradle due to the low tide, one was now always in readiness beside the Victoria Pier. The launch picked up eight bodies, some of them badly burned. They comprised four Chinese crew, three naval ratings and a maritime gunner from the Royal Artillery. The remains of another maritime gunner were picked up by the destroyer HMS *Ramsey*. These nine bodies were brought to Douglas and the Chinese and some of the others were buried in the Borough Cemetery, the rest being returned home for burial.

With the coming of spring, however, the renewed Allied offensive in the West pushed the German armies back to the borders of their homeland. As the final destruction of Nazi Germany drew near, one young Manx airman expressed what was perhaps a surprising view in a letter home. In it he stated that although the British people had waited for five years to see this systematic wiping out of the Third Reich, it would be a very hard person who didn't feel the tragedy of it. He added:

> One derives a certain satisfaction as of a job well done, but it's damned difficult not to feel pity. However, I think everybody regards it as an essential part of their discipline, comparable to standing your ground under fire, not to let these instinctive feelings stand in the way of their better judgment.[1]

Such views would probably have been shaken by the discovery and news broadcasts of the German concentration camp at Belsen, which was liberated by British troops on 15 April. An editorial in the *Isle of Man Times* expressed indignation that in spite of this, under the terms of the Geneva Convention to which Britain adhered, German prisoners of war were entitled to more rations than British civilians:

> There are prisoners of war in the Isle of Man. As you pass the barbed wire any day, do the men behind it look thin and exhausted? No fear! The race whose members committed

Members of the Manx Regiment with a captured German staff car near the Kiel Canal on VE Day. (Courtesy of the Manx Aviation Preservation Society/Manx Regiment Museum)

the atrocities at Buchenwald and Belsen and many another places, which has often treated its military prisoners most vilely, has no claim to be treated with generosity – and it is being generous when you go on observing the rules long

after the enemy has broken the whole set. The publication
of the Buchenwald horrors has awakened the British public
to our own national habit of 'softness'.[2]

Just over a week later the war in Europe was over. People on the Isle
of Man began celebrating on the evening of 7 May, in expectation
of the official statement of victory the following day. There were
reports of many servicemen, British and American, drinking a
toast to the defeat of Nazi Germany in Manx pubs, but relatively
little drunkenness. This was perhaps because a suggested extension
to licensing hours had been refused by the authorities. Other
celebrations the following day had a particularly Manx character.
As a child, Roy Holt of Bolton spent his holidays during the war
on the island and he recalled many years later the first turning of
the Laxey Wheel in almost six years:

> We used to stay in a hotel on Loch promenade, just round
> the corner from the Strand, run by a Mr and Mrs Critchley.
> My father had got friendly with the gentleman who was
> maintaining the wheel, who said that he was going to try
> and see if it would turn to celebrate VE day. He warned
> that the slate steps could be slippery and it would be at our
> own risk if we went up; my father sent my mother first, I
> followed and he came behind, it was quite a climb. On top
> the gentleman opened a hatch over the top of the tower; we
> could see the water rising up! He then lifted another hatch
> and we saw the water flowing along the trough under the
> platform; it overflowed into the paddleboxes, first one then
> two and into a third, then with a creak and a shudder the
> wheel started to turn. The people gathered below started
> cheering, I can still hear those cheers today; the day after
> was my sixth birthday, what a present!![3]

Back in Douglas, one of the most patriotic displays came from
the modest working-class homes of Chester Street. Besides an
exceptionally lavish display of flags and bunting, householders
in this small, narrow street painted the kerbstones in red, white,
and blue, and also painted patriotic mottos on the roadway. Frank
Cowin remembered that although the news was widely anticipated,
the announcement on the radio when it finally came still had

his family scrambling around looking for some bunting for the house. He also recalled a potentially far more serious incident that occurred later on VE Day, and which perhaps illustrates the way in which five years of war had made both soldiers and civilians alike careless about the dangers of explosives:

> They had a big fireworks-cum-bonfire at the bottom of Broadway and of course we went off along to that. [The troops] were throwing these fireworks about which actually were their thunderflashes, and they threw one; it wasn't doing anything and I picked it up. The chap that had thrown it shouted 'Drop it!' So I dropped it, and it went off just out of my hand. I had a corduroy-type jacket on; it singed the arm, blew the button off it, deafened and blinded me – temporarily – and it blew a chunk out of the heel of my hand, from which I still bear the scar. That was just hanging loose, which I didn't realise because the whole arm was numbed, and I was walking back to where the others were when they said 'Your hand's bleeding', and I had blood dripping off my fingers.[4]

Perhaps the celebrations were somewhat muted by the awareness that in the Far East, Japan remained still to be defeated and for military units it was still business as usual. By the end of May 1945 the resident instructional unit at Jurby had changed name yet again, to become known as No. 5 Air Navigation School, but life for the moment largely carried on as before. Training had subtly switched emphasis once more, with Avro Ansons

Frank Cowin (right) with his brother and sisters outside the family home on VE Day, 1945. (Courtesy of Frank Cowin)

Coastwatchers at their final stand-down parade in Douglas, summer 1945. Wearing a mixture of naval and army uniform, these men had kept a constant vigil along the Manx coast for five years. (Courtesy of Barry Bridson)

and Vickers Wellingtons now serving as flying equipment. In July 1945 the island welcomed Their Majesties King George VI and Queen Elizabeth, for whom there was a large turn-out. Many of the Douglas schoolchildren were at the Villa Marina to receive them, and the turn-out along the route was impressive, with many people waving flags. The royal party visited the Tynwald ceremony, and then went on to King William's College. Later they visited the south of the island and Port St Mary. It is reported, perhaps apocryphally, that the king while here heard that at Cregneash the Manx language was still spoken. He asked to hear some of it and the lieutenant governor, casting his eye hastily over the assembled crowd, is reputed to have spotted an elderly farmhand. He asked him if he could recite the Lord's Prayer in Manx for the king. 'I couldn't recite it in bloody English,' came the reply.

On the evening of 14 August news reached the island of the surrender of Japan, and the announcement that the following morning would be VJ Day. Although it was approaching midnight,

This advertisement from an August 1945 Manx newspaper makes reference to the atomic bomb 'adding the finishing touch'.

ships' horns were sounded at full strength and in various tones for about two hours; searchlights from naval ships lit up the sky and sea with rainbow colours, and rockets and Very lights provided a fireworks show; soon after there was added the peal of guns. The bell from HMS *Valkyrie* was rung constantly and a bonfire burned on the lower slopes of Douglas Head. The promenade swarmed with thousands of residents and holidaymakers. Some observers said the English people were more demonstrative than the Manx, but all were intensely happy. Long strings of excited young people marched up and down, singing all the old favourite music-hall songs like *Pack Up Your Troubles in Your Old Kit-Bag* and *It's a Long Way to Tipperary* or *Rolling Home*. People made little rings and danced; they rang handbells. A lad climbed to the top of the Jubilee Clock where he took off his light holiday vest and flung it down to the crowd. Two other lads danced on the top of the fountain in the Promenade gardens.

The town of Peel officially celebrated the victory over Japan in the afternoon and evening of 15 August, and though the event lacked the spontaneity of those of the first announcement victory, an enjoyable time was still given to both children and adults. During the afternoon the three halls in the town were transformed into efficient restaurants, and fed all the local children with tea, mineral waters and cakes. Afterwards the old people were entertained. Following the tea there was a picture show at the Pavilion Cinema, and an entertaining hour in the Albert Hall with Mr Howard Hugh and his team of rabbits, kittens and musical instruments, followed by community singing. During the evening the townspeople were entertained by the RAF Pipe Band from Jurby, and a firework display was given round a bonfire. Following this, the crowds moved along the promenade to the bottom of Stanley Road and spent some hectic hours dancing to the strains of the Peveril Melody Makers and thence adjourned for more dancing in the Albert Hall. The revelry continued until late into the night, and so the most destructive war in history came to an end.

Epilogue

In the immediate aftermath of the war there was a winding-down of the military presence on the island. At HMS *Urley* the final three Fleet Air Arm squadrons that were present, mainly operating Fairey Barracudas, disbanded in December 1945. Their base was finally paid off on 14 January 1946. As RAF Dalby formed an important component of the British early-warning network, it remained operational for a few years after the war before being mothballed. Today it is still well-preserved, with all the technical blocks still standing and put to farm use. No. 5 Air Navigation School left Jurby in September 1946, while No. 11 Air Gunners' School moved in from Andreas which was closing. Like Dalby, Jurby remained operational.

There had been no time in which to organize a 1946 TT, but that same month saw the first racing on the island in seven years as the Manx Grand Prix returned. Despite the fact that all riders were on inferior pool petrol and there were still restrictions on travel, the meeting was well-attended and the results keenly followed.

It took more time, however, for the island's tourist industry to get properly back on its feet. The Steam Packet Company embarked upon an immediate rebuilding programme to replace the ships that had been lost in the war, but it would be some years before this was achieved. Among those people who had been compulsorily removed from their homes or guest houses to provide accommodation for internees, bitterness over the way in which they had been treated lasted for decades. A particularly sore point was the matter of furniture. At the beginning of the war, tables, beds and other items in requisitioned guest houses had been hired by the British government, but midway through it had been compulsorily purchased. At the end of the war, the surviving furniture was stored at Derby Castle and boarding-house-keepers were invited to

Tourists at Sea Lion Rocks, Groudle, before the war. It was one of a number of tourist attractions on the island which had closed during the war and did not re-open afterwards. (Author's collection)

purchase back those items that were theirs. However, it turned out that those who arrived first got the best items and the rest whatever was left. It took some boarding-house-keepers several years before they could get their property – which was their livelihood – back up to the standard at which they could accept paying guests once again.

Many of the attractions that had closed for the duration of the war did not re-open again, notable examples being the Marine Drive tramway, the gypsy encampment on Douglas Head and the Groudle zoo. In the latter case this was perhaps no bad thing, for one commentator at the time wrote to a newspaper to note that: 'There used to be seals in Groudle Glen, and they were a great attraction to all the boys, who used to try and hit them with stones. There is nothing nice to see [in] freedom-loving animals caged behind iron bars.'[1]

In a classic case of missing the point, in an editorial comment the editor stated that this was an exaggeration and the seals were not a target for every boy who visited! Although Hall Caine airport would never re-open, Ronaldsway would become the island's main airport, the wartime infrastructure proving a boon to post-war commercial air travel.

Across Britain as a whole, shortages of some items actually became more severe after the war, and bread rationing was introduced to the island for the first time in July 1946. The wet summer and autumn of that year made life difficult for those who under wartime control had been forced to change the way in which they farmed their land. The drive for greater food production and state control of agriculture had hit the small landholders harder than the bigger ones. Adrian Wall wrote after the war:

> Our thoughts turned to the small Manx crop farmer whose income depends upon the sale of his crops, while others, whose farms have for generations proved their worth as good stock-breeding grass farms, have had to be turned into grain-producing units, for which purpose they may be totally unsuited. Many would not have sown a single ear if they had not been ordered to do so, as arable farming was not their lie of country; they were dairy farmers with an all-the-year-round income and grass as their sheet anchor. The risks and the gamble of cereals were not for them; they were for the bigger men with available capital. Today many are faced with ruin through the inclement weather.[2]

Dusty's cartoon from May 1947 shows a proud war veteran struggling to heat his home in the 'austerity Britain' of Clement Attlee's Labour government.

The legacy of state intervention in society continued, and the Isle of Man followed the UK in establishing a range of social security benefits as part of the welfare state envisaged by Sir William Beveridge. Although these reforms were an important part of what many in the armed forces believed they were fighting for and certainly this would do much to alleviate severe poverty on the island, it should not be imagined that it was universally welcomed. One correspondent wrote:

> The Social Services Bill...will...prove to be the most insane conglomeration ever conceived outside a madhouse. It may appear strange to some readers why Manxland's electorate-chosen non-Labour representatives should so blindly support such a communistic scheme. This is due presumably to their being misguided... Sir William, although supposedly Liberal, conceived a scheme (Social

HMS Manxman, *the warship paid for by the Isle of Man. (Author's collection)*

Services) whereby one half of Britain should live upon the other half... The adoption of Sir William's scheme, which out-Herods Herod, makes him a super-Socialist or Labourite.[3]

There was a succession of VIP visits in the immediate post-war years, with that of General Sir Brian Horrocks being followed by HMS *Manxman*, the island's adopted warship. Her crew brought with them a number of gifts including a Japanese sword from the surrender ceremony in Tokyo bay. In 1948 Field Marshal Montgomery visited the Isle of Man to receive the freedom of Douglas. Many ex-servicemen, particularly those who fought under him in the desert, lined his route as he toured the island.

These men, who had been away from home for in some cases four or five years in the armed forces, had to adjust once more to civilian life and ways. Unemployment was seldom an issue; Bob Quayle, for example, returned home on an afternoon boat and was back on the farm the following morning, but he found that as in every town and city in Britain, divisions existed in his village after the war between those who had seen active service and those who had not. Quayle remembered the tensions this caused and spoke candidly about them:

> It was a farming community. I left the plough; they hid behind the plough... There was a damn big divide after the war. You hear people saying, 'Oh my Dad never spoke about it.' But it wasn't because their dad didn't want to speak about it, because if you did speak about it you were pushed to one side. If you were in a pub, and you mentioned the war, you'd empty the pub. There was that many that didn't go, you'd empty the pub. It got to be so you didn't mention the war, you didn't dare talk about it or you'd be asked to leave. You had to meet up with somebody who

A life-ring, presented among other gifts by the crew of the Manxman *during her 1946 visit. (Courtesy of Manx National Heritage)*

had been. If you met somebody who'd been you could have
a chat, but nobody else wanted to know.[4]

He remained convinced, nevertheless, that his decision to join
the army had been the right one, a conviction shared by many
ex-servicemen. For some there was a physical legacy of the war.
When Allen Martin of Ramsey died suddenly in 1951, his death
was attributed to the fact that ten years previously when in the
Royal Navy his ship had been sunk and he had been in the water
for some time, ingesting oil. His obituary noted that he had
suffered considerably in the years that followed. Others lived with
the physical reminders of their service, but often overcame any
limitations these imposed. Howard Simcocks had been blinded
while serving as an officer in North Africa, but by using braille
was able to pass his law exams and become a successful advocate.
There were many in the 1950s, however, who would leave the island
for the better employment opportunities offered by the United
Kingdom or Australia.

Politically, Deemster Percy Cowley had been correct when
he had observed that wartime changes might have long-lasting
effects. The Executive Council that was established following
the 1949 Manx General Election was the executive body of the
island's government, and would eventually become the Council
of Ministers. It was the successor to an Executive Committee of
Tynwald that was set up in 1946, and this in turn grew directly from
the Tynwald War Committee. Although a letter from the Home
Office in 1946 stated that the role of the Executive Committee
was 'to assist the Lieutenant Governor in the performance of his
duties', ultimately the lieutenant governor would be replaced as
its chairman by an elected member. The chairman would in later
years become known as the chief minister, and like the conflict that
preceded it, the Second World War was a milestone on the long
road to full Manx democracy.

Howard Simcocks, who was blinded while on active service but who went on to pass his law exams using braille. (Courtesy of the Manx Aviation Preservation Society/Manx Regiment Museum)

Endnotes

Chapter 1:

1. *Green Final*, 21 October 1939.

Chapter 2:

1. *Isle of Man Examiner*, 28 June 1940.
2. www.website.lineone.net/~tom_lee/monas%20isle%20hms.htm
3. Ibid.
4. *Isle of Man Times*, 24 August 1940.
5. *Starshell*, Vol. 7, No. 43, Summer 2008, pp.16–20.
6. Ibid.
7. Ibid.
8. Account courtesy of Harry Martland.
9. Manx National Heritage, Tom Helsby papers, MS 11490.
10. Manx National Heritage, Radcliffe Duggan, MS 11490.
11. Ibid.
12. Account courtesy of Junemary Moyle.
13. Manx National Heritage, Bill Sleigh, MS 09538.
14. Manx National Heritage, Thomas Cannell, MS 10016.
15. *Country Life*, 19 February 1981.
16. Manx National Heritage, Thomas Cannell, MS 10016.
17. Manx National Heritage, Tom Corteen, MS 09538.
18. Manx National Heritage, Bill Sleigh, MS 09538.
19. Ibid.
20. Account courtesy of Audrey Mansell.
21. *Isle of Man Times*, 27 July 1940.
22. IOMPRO 29749/70, Minutes of the War Committee, folder 1.
23. Manx National Heritage, MS 12388.
24. Charles Forte, *Autobiography*, London, 1986, p.45.
25. Terry Cringle, conversation with author.
26. *Ramsey Courier*, 9 August 1940.
27. *Isle of Man Times*, 19 October 1940.
28. *Ramsey Courier*, 13 December 1940.
29. *Ramsey Courier*, 20 December 1940.

Chapter 3:

1. *Isle of Man Examiner*, 31 January 1941.
2. Manx National Heritage, Edward Winter Anstey, MS 12217.
3. *Isle of Man Examiner*, 12 September 1989.
4. Manx National Heritage, SA 0529.
5. John Charnley, *Blackshirts and Roses*, London, 1990, p.132.
6. Hector Emmanuelli, *A Sense of Belonging*, Lagenfeld, 2010, p.78.
7. www.sstohms.co.uk/valkyrie1.htm
8. *Isle of Man Times*, 2 February 1946.
9. Jon Pertwee, *Moon Boots and Dinner Suits*, London, 1984, p.183.
10. *Isle of Man Examiner*, 5 September 1941.
11. *Isle of Man Examiner*, 22 August 1941.
12. *Ramsey Courier*, 12 September 1941.
13. www.mike-caine.com/howstrake-the-war-years
14. www.exroyalmarinesbandsmen.net/IOM3.htm
15. Manx National Heritage, Syd Cringle, MS 13229.

Chapter 4:

1. Manx National Heritage, MS 10423.
2. Manx National Heritage, Bruce Toothill, MS 09674.
3. Gordon Cowley, conversation with author.
4. Ibid.
5. *Isle of Man Examiner*, 2 July 1943.
6. www.culturevannin.im/media//Oral%20History/Transcripts/Briggs_Laura%20Mrs.pdf
7. Ann Moore, *Me and Ellan Vannin*, Worcester, 2014, p.26.
8. Frank Cowin, conversation with author.
9. Manx National Heritage, Syd Cringle, MS 13229.
10. *Isle of Man Examiner*, 14 November 1941.
11. *Ramsey Courier*, 14 August 1942.
12. *Isle of Man Examiner*, 20 November 1942.
13. *Isle of Man Times*, 3 October 1942.
14. Adrian Wall, *Cardles Farm Again*, London, Kaye-Wood, 1945, p.133.
15. *Isle of Man Times*, 5 December 1942.

Chapter 5:

1. Toni Onley and Gregory Strong, *Flying Colours: The Toni Onley Story*, Madeira Park, 2002, p.41.
2. Manx National Heritage, MS 10500.
3. Nikolai Giovannelli, *Paper Hero*, Douglas, 1970, p.55.

4. *Isle of Man Examiner*, 2 July 1943.
5. *Isle of Man Times*, 7 August 1943.
6. Giovannelli, op cit, p.58.
7. *Isle of Man Times*, 25 December 1943.
8. *Isle of Man Examiner*, 28 January 1944.

Chapter 6:

1. www.thememoryproject.com/stories/1305:frank-p.o.-tel-bowen
2. *Isle of Man Examiner*, 19 May 1944.
3. Frank Cowin, conversation with author.
4. Ibid.
5. Adrian Wall, *Cardles Farm Once More*, Ramsey, sd p.9.
6. *Isle of Man Times*, 28 August 1954.
7. Eric Cain, conversation with author.
8. Ibid.
9. Ibid.
10. Hector Duff, conversation with author.
11. Joan Roylance, conversation with author.
12. Manx National Heritage, MS 11398.
13. Martin Bowman, *So Near and Yet So Far*, Barnsley, 2013, p.82.
14. Bowman, op cit, p.142.
15. *Isle of Man Examiner*, 22 December 1944.

Chapter 7:

1. *Isle of Man Times*, 24 March 1945.
2. *Isle of Man Times*, 28 April 1945.
3. Roy Holt, correspondence with author.
4. Frank Cowin, conversation with author.

Epilogue:

1. *Isle of Man Examiner*, 19 July 1946.
2. Adrian Wall, *Cardles Farm Once More*, p.135.
3. *Ramsey Courier*, 9 April 1948.
4. Bob Quayle, conversation with author.

Bibliography

Primary sources:

Bowman, Martin, *So Near and Yet So Far* (Barnsley, Pen & Sword, 2013)

Charnley, John, *Blackshirts and Roses* (London, Blackhouse, 1990)

Emanuelli, Hector, *A Sense of Belonging* (Langenfeld, 2010)

Forte, Charles, *Autobiography* (London, Sedgwick, 1986)

Giovannelli, Nikolai, *Paper Hero* (Douglas, Island Development Co., 1970)

Moore, Ann, *Me and Ellan Vannin* (Worcester, Eyelevel Books, 2014)

Onley, Toni and Strong, Gregory, *Flying Colours: The Toni Onley Story* (Madeira Park, British Columbia, Harbour Publishing, 2002)

Pertwee, Jon, *Moon Boots and Dinner Suits* (London, 1984)

Wall, Adrian, *Cardles Farm Again* (London, Kaye Wood, 1945)

Wall, Adrian, *Cardles Farm Once More* (Ramsey, Gansey Publications, sd)

Secondary sources (newspapers):

Isle of Man Examiner

Isle of Man Times

Peel City Guardian

Ramsey Courier

Index